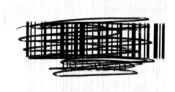

# WHEN
# LIFE
# GETS
# HARD...

AUDIO PRODUCTS BY MEG JOHNSON:

*When Life Gets Hard . . .*

# WHEN
# LIFE
# GETS
# HARD...

# Meg Johnson

Covenant Communications, Inc.

For Whit

# Acknowledgments

THIS BOOK WOULD NOT HAVE been possible without my husband, whose patience and support give wings to my crazy ideas.

I would like to thank my mom and dad, who loved me enough to let me fly solo so I could have important life experiences worthy to include in this book.

I would like to thank Phil Reschke for believing in me and providing me with the opportunity to share my experiences with a broader audience.

I would like to thank my editor, Samantha Van Walraven, and the entire Covenant Communications team for their efforts and expertise in polishing this book.

# CLOSING THE GAPS

I MOVED TO UTAH WHEN I was fourteen and shook my head in dismay as we drove to our new house nestled in the foothills of Utah's mountains—Utah's brown, ugly mountains. They were such a stark contrast to the evergreen, pine-covered mountains I'd left behind in Idaho. It took many years before I grew to love those brown mountains, but looking at them now, I can't believe I ever disliked them to begin with.

Every day when I was in junior high, high school, and college, I looked at those mountains. I skied them, hiked them, snowboarded and snow-shoed on them, swam and climbed trees, ran from snakes, and played some serious games of capture-the-flag in them. I have never found a waterslide that could compete with one particular mountain pond and rope swing in those mountains.

I might not have been born in Utah, but I grew up in the foothills of its brown mountains.

In my travels, I've noticed that just like Idaho is green and Utah is brown, other places have their own colors too. I've slept on the beach of the Atlantic Ocean and awakened to silver waters. I've driven through the city of Hamburg and seen all its shades of gray. I've hiked the tallest peak in Massachusetts and looked out over the yellow treetops. And if the rainbow has an end, it's in the tulip fields of Belgium. But I'd never seen anything red until I was twenty-two and took a trip to St. George.

I went with my friend Anton to see his little sister be baptized; it was my first time in Southern Utah, and I was spellbound by how beautiful everything looked—the red rocks, the red sand, the red dirt.

It was so different from Northern Utah; who would have thought that the same state could be so varied?

Awhile after we got there, Anton and I went for a walk through the red terrain behind his parents' home. Anton's sister's baptism wasn't for a couple of hours, so we searched for box turtles, lizards, and any other desert creature we could find. But it seemed that the only "creatures" around were mountain bikers and rock climbers. The red dirt path we were on forked, and Anton went one way to watch some rock climbers, and I went the other way to check out a large grouping of giant red boulders. There were a number of them all squished tightly together. They looked like the marshmallows you put on top of yams at Thanksgiving—you know, right after you take the yams out of the oven and the marshmallows are all puffy and toasty and squished into each other? That's what the boulders looked like, and I began to jump from boulder to boulder.

My shoes, I quickly discovered, had super grip on the soles. I felt like a spider, catching the end of my shoe on a boulder and being stable and secure enough to push off to get to another landing place. It felt cool to be so limitless. It felt cool to be so powerful. It felt cool to play with nature.

But it definitely wasn't cool outside; I actually felt hot. So I took off my olive-green zip-up jacket and threw it aside. It landed in a crumpled heap on the rocks as I continued to jump from one boulder to another . . .

To another.

And then I jumped for one last boulder . . . and it was the last time I ever jumped.

That last jump landed me in a wheelchair, unable to walk or use my hands. In the years that have followed, I've found truth and hope from Elder Neal A. Maxwell, who said, "[God] is a loving Father who wants us to have the happiness that results not from mere innocence but from proven righteousness. Therefore, he will, at times, not deflect the harsh learning experiences that may come to each of us—even though he will help us in coping with them."[1] And sometimes, these "harsh learning experiences" are just that—harsh.

Like me in red-rock St. George, all of us walk our path each day. And each day brings a new terrain and different curves on a familiar path. Our "strait and narrow" doesn't equate to "smooth and easy." At different times, our path gets rocky. At other times, our path gets *really* rocky. And at our worst times, it feels as if we're walking barefoot through shattered glass. Each path—yours and mine—weaves different routes through the highs and lows of life.

The rocky times in life happen despite our great efforts to avoid them. As long as we keep walking down our path, we will be challenged—physically, emotionally, mentally, and spiritually. It is difficult to continue on a straight course along our path, partly because the rough patches seem unbearable and partly because *off* the trail seems so much more enticing. *Off* the trail seems easier. Better. Nicer. Smoother.

But as smooth as *off* the trail seems and as tempted as we are to relieve ourselves of the difficulties of our path, we can't go near it. We must remain on our path because looming dangerously close to the edge of our path is not soft sand to rest our feet but rather gaps between the rocks. And if we fall into these gaps, something worse than physical damage will occur.

I know about gaps, and I know about falls. I've fallen figuratively, and I've fallen literally. They are both hard. But when I took my one last jump for a red-rock boulder in St. George, it opened the door for many figurative falls, even though that time my fall was literal.

By accident, when I jumped for that one last boulder in St. George, I jumped off a cliff.

I didn't even know I was near a cliff! But there I was, flying through the air, in a gap that distanced me from my path.

The boulder I had jumped for wasn't there. What I didn't understand then about the beautiful red-rock terrain of St. George was that all the red rocks and the red sand and the red dirt made everything blend together. The candy yam boulders that appeared

---

1   "Talk of the Month," *New Era*, May 1971.

to be squished together were actually separated by canyons and ravines—gaps.

When I jumped off the cliff, time slowed as I hung in the air. I was so surprised that I laughed. I mean, what else could I really do? I couldn't believe what had just happened. The realization hit me, and aloud I said, "I'm gonna fall!" I shut my eyes really tight, and I fell.

I don't remember the fall; I had the initial sensation of dropping, but that's all. I woke up facedown in the sand to the sound of my friend frantically calling my name. It turned out that when he came to look for me, he found my sweater on the boulders above. Looking down the thirty-five-foot drop, he panicked when he saw my still body and ran down the trail to where I lay.

I opened my eyes when I heard his voice, and I thought that maybe I had died. I wasn't dead, but I was close. I had broken both femurs, both wrists, my left collarbone, and four vertebrae in my neck. Remarkably, the only pain I had was on the palms of my hands; they had a rug-burn hurt coursing through them. I was life-flighted to a hospital in Salt Lake City, where I was diagnosed with a spinal cord injury that rendered me a quadriplegic. I was paralyzed from the chest down and didn't have use of my rock-scraped hands.

The doctors told me I would never walk again. I would never run or dance or use chopsticks. There is no cure for a spinal cord injury like mine.

I am paralyzed for the rest of my life. Until the day I die, I will use a wheelchair. I can't move or feel my legs. My stomach muscles don't work, and I can't sit unaided unless I carefully balance myself. When I lean over in my wheelchair to pick up the newspaper from the porch, I have to squeeze it with both hands because my fingers won't work to grab it. I then have to put it in my mouth and push myself back up to sitting position with my arms because my back muscles don't work to pull me back up.

It takes me a lot of extra time to do normal, everyday things. It takes me thirty full minutes to make a bed. It takes me almost three full minutes to get into the car. I have to use both hands to brush my teeth.

It is difficult to be physically paralyzed.

But as hard as it is for me to be physically paralyzed every day, it is *nothing* compared to what happens to us when we allow ourselves to become *spiritually* paralyzed!

Spiritual paralysis happens to us when we take side steps off the gospel path. These side steps can be sins committed or righteousness omitted in our everyday lives. And when we veer off the path, we come closer to the surrounding gaps in the rock, where Satan and his cronies lie in wait. They will reach up and grab us, and they won't hesitate to tell us we're not good enough, we're not smart enough, we're not nice enough, we're not talented enough, we're not *enough*—and they will pull on us until we fall and become spiritually paralyzed.

*Spiritual Paralysis*

Being spiritually paralyzed is much like being physically paralyzed, only worse.

A lot worse.

In my wheelchair, I can't feel a lot of my body. As a quadriplegic, I have little to no sensation from my armpits to my toes. A short time after I was paralyzed, a few six-year-old girls were crowding around me, leaning on my lap as they asked me about my body and what I could and couldn't feel. They touched my legs. "Can you feel that?"

I told them I couldn't.

They touched my stomach. "Can you feel *that*?"

I said no.

One little girl poked me in the eye and asked, "Whoa! Did you feel that?"

As I rubbed my watery, sore eye, one of the girls looked sideways at me and furrowed her brows in disbelief before saying, "You can't feel your legs at all? What if we stabbed them?"

As difficult as it is to imagine, it's true. I can't feel my legs, even if you stab them. Being numb to the world around me is weird. I mean, I spent twenty-two years being able to feel everything normally, and now I'm unable to feel most of my body. When I let my feet hang off my wheelchair bar and down to the grass, I crave the feeling of the grassy tickle, but it won't come for me.

I'm unsure if I'll ever be able to get used to not feeling with my physical senses.

But as strange and difficult as it is to not feel my physical world, it is nothing compared to what happens when Satan pulls us into the surrounding gaps. When we become spiritually paralyzed, our feelings become muted—we can no longer feel the sweet peace of the Spirit or the loving arms of the Savior. We block out the soul-tickling sensations we get when we receive divine guidance and inspiration. When we allow ourselves to fall into the gaps that surround the path, we choose to become spiritually numb.

Because I am numb and can't move, I am weak. As hard as I try, I am always slow. Likewise, being spiritually paralyzed weakens us. We will feel physically fatigued, and our strength for wholesome things will severely diminish. We tend to want to do less.

I do less because I can't stand, so I sit in my wheelchair. I am shorter than most others. I find that's true with spiritual paralysis too. We feel significantly smaller than those around us. Our confidence is lessened, and our ambitions cease.

When I was first paralyzed, my family, as you can imagine, was very sad. I soon discovered how much my accident had affected them. They cried and came to the hospital to visit me every day. Because I had breathing treatments around the clock, I couldn't communicate with them for many months, even though I tried. If we allow ourselves to become spiritually paralyzed, we will discover how many other problems it causes, not only for us but for those around us who love us. From my long experience in the hospital and watching my family cry, I can confirm that paralysis—of any kind—hurts others more than it hurts us.

### How Do We Become Spiritually Paralyzed?

Being spiritually "able" requires very simple steps—the kind of answers always given in Primary. Praying, reading scriptures, and being nice to others all invite the Holy Ghost and spiritual ability. Likewise, spiritual paralysis happens with similar simplicity.

Seemingly small sins of omission—like sleeping through church, skipping Sunday School, not going to the temple, and forgetting our own individual worth—bring us closer to the edge of the path and leave us unaided, unguarded, and vulnerable to Satan's pulls.

Seemingly small sins of commission jump us right off the edge and into spiritual paralysis. Anything that creates an unwholesome and unclean environment will drive away the Holy Spirit, allowing Satan to pull us down into spiritual paralysis. "Small" sins, like one teensy-weensy swear word, a passive-aggressive insult, or an off-color joke, are not tolerated by the Spirit, and He will leave. Satan will waste no time filling that vacancy and pulling us down into spiritual paralysis.

A lot is required from those who stay on this path, and the gaps can sometimes seem appealing. It appears to be more fun to venture off our path and skip church (just this once). It seems easier to rest our feet on the soft sand next to the gap and just lean over a tiny bit to share juicy gossip with our friends—it can even seem easier to rest by the gap's edge with our "friends" than to continue walking down our path through the rough stones and to try to keep that gossip inside us when it's just too good to go unsaid.

I was once at a bridal shower with many strong, active members of the Church. As the party progressed, I found myself stuck in a serious gossip circle. Every guest loudly shared their belittling opinions about someone they all knew. I stayed quiet and tried to ignore their remarks. After a while, my silence apparently made some of them uncomfortable, and one guest cut through all the gossipy chatter and said that everyone had better stop talking because they were making me feel bad. All the shower guests turned to me and tried to convince me that this person deserved their criticism. I didn't know what to say. It was hard to stay on the path because it would have been much easier to simply take a tiny step off and agree with them—they were all staring at me! After all, the person wasn't even there.

But being spiritually paralyzed is not a disability I can handle. I could not join in their gossip circle. Even if I'd known whom they were talking about, I would not have joined in. I am physically paralyzed, and I just can't afford to lose any more feeling, especially when it's the feeling of the Holy Ghost—and He never gossips.

Those who are spiritually disabled look at us as "self-righteous" and "haughty" when we refuse to join them in their unfair judgments, gossip, parties, movies, and every other activity that would numb us spiritually. They wallow selfishly in their spiritual paralysis. They know where the path is but choose to stay spiritually disabled. They do not wish to join us and, instead, despise us for our valiance and humility—and *ability*.

### What Can We Do?

Staying spiritually able is the only ability necessary to continue down the path, but Satan continues to remind us how difficult it is to remain there. To keep our spiritual abilities, we must close the gaps around us and trap Satan and all his followers in the ravines. If he is trapped down there, we are free to travel down our path in peace, knowing that he most surely cannot reach up and bring us down to spiritual paralysis.

Closing the gaps is difficult; it takes daily focus and hard work. To close the gaps, think of G-A-P-S—Gratitude, Attitude, Prayer, and Service. Each of these will squish the gaps together, tighter and tighter, and we can focus on the path, no matter how difficult it may be.

We must start with the very basic first step of being grateful. It is our first step, not because it starts with a *G* (I could have thought of something else) but because we are often too weak to begin with anything else.

We are sometimes too emotionally beaten from the stresses of life or too socially beaten to muster an "I can do it" attitude. In those weak times (and even as preparation against those times), we must start with being grateful.

The Lord's will is that we are thankful first. The prophet Alma taught, "When thou risest in the morning let thy heart be full of thanks unto God."[2] We have been counseled to give thanks as our very first act of each day. Gratitude gives us strength and makes it easier for us to have a good outlook for the rest of the day.

---

2    Alma 37:37.

I have seen the effects of being grateful, not only in my life but also in the lives of others. For a semester in college, I carpooled with my little brother. He is two years younger than I am, and we were both attending Weber State University. To make it to our first class on time, we had to start traveling at seven in the morning. Both of us were tired and groggy.

We made it a goal to not turn on the radio and listen to any music until we reached a certain overpass bridge that was the halfway point between our house and the school. As we drove without music, we each took turns sharing things we were grateful for.

I was usually a little more awake and bubbly in the mornings than my night-owl brother, and I shared the things I was grateful for, like rainbows and stars and fresh-cut grass. My brother's more surly expressions of gratitude were for "that one guy's roof" and "that mailbox" and, referring to me, "that you only talk *some* of the time."

Our little exercise lasted only ten minutes or so, but I started to notice a difference in myself on the days we did it. I was happier, and my schoolwork did not seem too difficult or overwhelming. I seemed to be fresher, more alert, more awake, and more involved in the day's activities.

Likewise, I began to observe the same happenings in my brother. He was more alert and "awake." He smiled more. He told more jokes and was less sarcastic. I saw the truth of the scripture in Doctrine and Covenants that promises "he who receiveth all things with thankfulness shall be made glorious; and the things of this earth shall be added unto him, even an hundred fold, yea, more."[3] As we were thankful for the everyday things, we felt glorious. We received the "things of this earth" that the scripture promises to those who are thankful. We received joy and involvement throughout our day, just for being grateful. We had "more."

I see gratitude as a kind of reverse psychology. When we are grateful for what we have, we get more, "even an hundred fold" more. But it isn't always easy to be grateful. President David O.

---

3    D&C 78:19.

McKay said, "We find in the bitter chill of adversity the *real* test of our gratitude."[4]

I endured a huge test of my gratitude after I accidentally jumped off the red-rock cliff and was brought to the hospital, where, after many surgeries, my lungs collapsed.

To keep me breathing, the doctors placed an intubation tube down my throat. The intubation tube is very much like a blue rubber garden hose. It went into my mouth and down my throat and then branched out into my lungs. My mouth was always open around this blue rubber hose that attached to a very large machine, which kept the rhythm of the airflow constant. This tube breathed for me, but my lungs continued to fill with fluid and then collapse, so the doctors stuck tubes in my chest so my lungs could drain.

In addition to these breathing support tubes, I had many others. I had a tube going into my nose that fed me and a tube going into my elbow pit that watered me, as well as PICC lines for medication in my upper arms. Each tube was taped to my skin with postcard-sized pieces of tape.

My motionless body lay on the hospital bed with life-giving blue and white and blood-filled tubing escaping out from under both sides of the white sheet that covered me. I have no pictures to share with you. The scene, my family tells, was too horrific to even consider photographing. Their daughter, sister, and friend lay beneath all those artificial life-supports, unable to speak or laugh or eat or drink.

Lying helpless in the hospital was the rockiest road I have ever traveled.

Sometimes our lives become rockier than we think we can bear. We wonder how we can ever make it through—it seems there is no remedy. Even though you may not have ever kept still in a hospital bed, tied down with tubes and machines, I know that in your own way you have also been to this seventh circle of

---

4   *Pathways to Happiness,* comp. Llewelyn R. McKay, [Salt Lake City: Bookcraft, 1957], 318; emphasis added.

hopelessness. And I may sound a little gloomy, but I know that you will visit that despair again in your life. We all do. It is what we were excited to do before we came to this earth.

In that sorrow-soaked hospital room, I woke up one morning. The radio and television were off, and the room was quiet, except for the constant beeps of the machines. I scanned the room and saw that my family and friends were gone. I looked down the bed at the white sheets and mass of tubing spidering out from the edges of the bed. I tried to look out the door and down the hall to see if I could see anyone, but there was no one there. Not even a nurse.

I started to cry.

I cried for myself and the pathetic situation I was in. I cried because I was scared. I cried because I was confused. I cried because I felt alone. And each cry was a side step off my path and into the gap. Being physically paralyzed was not good enough for Satan; he wanted me to be spiritually paralyzed as well. If he could convince me to give in to hopelessness, he could achieve dual paralysis. And there is no life-support for the spiritually paralyzed. We either walk with God, or we don't.

Walking with God is the only kind of walking I care to do.

I tried to stop the tears from flowing freely down my tape-covered face. I tried to be brave. I tried to be strong. I tried to be happy. I tried, but I was not strong enough. I was too weak physically, emotionally, and mentally, to rally any real determination.

In despair, I opened my eyes again and stared at the ceiling. I said in my heart, *Heavenly Father, please give me love for that ceiling.*

And my heart fluttered.

My eyes crossed the room, and I looked out the window as I prayed more. *Heavenly Father, please bless me with love for that window.* And my heart fluttered again.

I stared through the window and into the parking garage across the street. *Heavenly Father, please bless me with love for that car.* My mouth twitched into a sort of smile as my gaze came back into the room, and I named more things.

*Heavenly Father, please bless me with love for that chair and that television and that light switch. Bless me with love for that wall and those get-well cards and the buttons on the wall. Bless me with love for those balloons and these white sheets and this tube. Bless me with love for my casts and my lifeless legs.*

I named everything around the room that I could see until I had named all that there was to name. And when there was nothing left to ask to love, I laid in silence. I felt my heart inside my chest beat rhythmically as it seemed to carry me higher, even seeming to lift me off the bed. My eyes closed as I felt the weight of the room release from me, and I seemed to hover above the bed in a cloud. Tears spilled down my taped face—for a different reason this time—and I smiled.

A respiratory therapist came to my bedside and began to adjust the intubation tube so she could fill my lungs with medications. Usually, I would have closed my eyes and tried to ignore her, as this was an uncomfortable happening, but that day, I could not. I stared at her, willing her to look at me. My forehead was covered with bandages and my mouth had tubes and my nose had tubes and all anyone could see on my face were my eyes peering between masses of medical equipment, but still I stared. I needed her to know how good it felt to be me.

This is the power of love. In several languages, *love* is used in the expression of gratitude. In English, sometimes I feel as if it is the same, not with the words but with the feelings used as I express love or gratitude. As I expressed my love for the items in the room around me, it was as if I were saying thank you to each one. Thank you for just being there. From this experience, I conclude that gratitude from the mouth is "thank you," but gratitude from the heart is "I love you."

A quadriplegic without the use of his arms, hands, legs, or body at all, said, "Attitude makes all the difference, but gratitude brings me joy."[5] As we begin our rocky journey to close the gaps, we must begin with gratitude for what we have. Even—and especially—when it feels as if we have nothing left to be thankful for.

---

5    S. Seegmiller; used with permission.

Sometimes people feel there is little to be grateful for. All they can see is the bad, and then worse things continue to happen to them—their car breaks down . . . again, their newspaper is soaked, no one calls on their birthday. Some may think their life is much too awful to have anything to be grateful for—but these people are very mistaken.

Being grateful for the things we have is different from having things to be grateful for. In the hospital, with tubes in my lungs, arms, and nose, I found basic items to love and be thankful for: a chair, a window, and a light switch. And in that hospital, when I didn't have anything—not even the ability to breathe by myself—I was grateful for everything.

No matter what we have or don't have in this life, we can be grateful. Gratitude doesn't mean that we have things; it means only that we're grateful for what we have. There is always something to be grateful for.

Making long lists of things we are grateful for can be good, and it will help us through extremely rough patches along the trail. However, expressing our gratitude only in this way is the equivalent of eating a week's worth of food at once. Time-wise, it makes sense; I mean, we *have* to eat that much anyway, so why not just do it all at once and get it over with? But cramming all our food in will make us feel sick for one day (maybe two . . .) and hungry for all the others. And just like our food, gratitude is not a weekly or biweekly or "in-times-of-need," all-at-once activity. Creating lengthy lists of our blessings, while fun, will take a lot of time out of our already busy days and will soon wear us out. If we feel like we should create a long list of things we're grateful for, we've likely been gratitude starved.

A healthy way to express gratitude to our Heavenly Father is consistently throughout the day. We will feel "full" as we express gratitude in our morning prayers, to our family, while driving our car, on our bikes, in our gardens, and to our neighbors. As we are constantly grateful, we will rarely feel hungry for the Spirit; He will fill us. Through hard times, though, we may be a little hungrier for the Spirit, and making a long gratitude list "snack" will fill us back up.

Cicero, one of the greatest philosophers from ancient Rome, taught this profound truth: "Gratitude is not only the greatest of virtues, but the parent of all the others."[6] When we start our daily journey by being grateful and carrying gratitude with us throughout our day, we strengthen our hearts against the adversary and begin our everyday effort to close the gaps, eliminating Satan's whispered entreaties that there is little in our lives that can make us happy.

As we fill our hearts with the Holy Spirit and thankfulness, we soften the rocks beneath our feet, which will take the edge off our sorest trials. With our focus on our blessings, we're strong enough to move to the second step in closing our gaps.

---

6     Roman author, orator, and politician (106 BC–43 BC), http://www. quotationspage.com/quote/4074.html.

# ATTITUDE

EVERY WEEK, I WATCH THE young women in my ward stand and repeat the Young Women theme: "We are daughters of our Heavenly Father, who loves us." What a wonderful reminder of who we are. If I could have one wish for the world, it would be that every person would say this every morning: *I am a child of my Heavenly Father, who loves me.*

On the day that I was paralyzed and flown to a hospital in Salt Lake City, the prophet Gordon B. Hinckley was there visiting his wife. Even though he was busy with personal matters, he took the time to come into my hospital room and give me a blessing. I was in and out of consciousness and don't remember most of what was said, but I will never forget one message. I also know that if he could have come to your house to bless you, he would have told you the exact same thing he told me when he put his hands on my head. "Jesus Christ knows where you are. He knows what has happened to you, and He knows what will happen to you."

We are sons and daughters of our Heavenly Father. He and His Son, Jesus Christ, are keenly aware of where we are and what we are doing. They knew us before we came to earth, and They know us now. With so many people in the world, I often wonder how my little problems and struggles could rank very high on any divine "importance scale," but Heavenly Father has shown me again and again that I matter. I love how author C. S. Lewis describes our personal relationship with the Lord: "He has infinite attention to spare for each one of us. He does not have to deal with us in the mass. You are as much alone with Him as if you were the only being He had ever created."[7]

---

7   *Mere Christianity,* [New York: HarperCollins, 1952], 168.

C. S. Lewis was not a prophet, but I believe he correctly described the manner in which God attends to each of us. He knows where we are, what we need to do here, and where we are going, and He wants to help us on our journey! He wants us to close the gaps, starting with being grateful for the blessings He has already given us and continuing to remember where we came from, why we are here, and where we are going—He wants us to have not just a good attitude but an *eternal* attitude.

Keeping an eternal attitude is often hard to do. Hardships and challenges overcome us, and our efforts to do good and be good seem unrecognized as we trudge through life.

Each day we have new and old struggles that make our lives difficult—familiar and unfamiliar rocks beneath our feet. We have work, we have chores, and we have little time to do things we enjoy. Sometimes our trials are even worse than normal, and we have to manage feelings of loneliness, longing, and despair.

I have a motto: *When life gets too hard to stand, just keep on rollin'!* Obviously, this motto applies to me because my life is literally too hard to stand in, but in my wheelchair, I keep on rolling. But I know this motto is just as applicable for you as it is for me. You don't have to be in a wheelchair to know what it feels like when life becomes too hard to stand. We all have challenges and trials and disabilities to deal with, and the worst ones are those we can't see. They are the ones inside—the ones we all have. As unappealing as these trials are, I know Heavenly Father wants us to have them.

As you can imagine, it was difficult for my family to hear the doctor tell them I would be paralyzed for the rest of my life. It was hard for each member of my family, but it was particularly hard for my little brother, who was seventeen at the time. He and I had danced together in a dance company, and later on he told me that after hearing my prognosis from the doctor on that first day at the hospital, he went home and shut himself in his bedroom and prayed. He prayed for the one thing any one of us would go home and pray for if this happened to someone we love. "Heavenly Father, please don't make Meg do this," he said. "Give it to me."

He told me he prayed for quite some time, repeating his prayer over and over, until he heard an answer. The Holy Spirit came to his heart and *chastised* him, asking, *What gives you the right to take away her challenges?* President Howard W. Hunter said that "life—every life—has a full share of ups and downs. Indeed, we see many joys and sorrows in the world, many changed plans and new directions, many blessings that do not always look or feel like blessings."[8] These challenges and trials are gifts from our Heavenly Father to help us become more like Him—and we were excited to have them!

When was the last time you were so excited about something that you actually shouted? Well, when we learned about the plan of salvation from our Father in Heaven, we were so excited that we shouted for joy![9]

I know we were all excited to come to earth to get a body. When I got my patriarchal blessing, I was told that when I was in the premortal existence, I loved the plan of our Heavenly Father. I was so excited that I even shared my feelings with other spirits and urged them to accept our Father's plan. I had faith in Heavenly Father's promise that mortality would be a wonderful experience because we were in the process of becoming like our heavenly parents. And I know you were just as excited!

But our excitement in heaven was not only for the fun, happy things we would find on earth. We were also excited to experience the *sad* things. We were just as excited to cry as we were to laugh.

After I was paralyzed, I spent quite a long time in the hospital. One long night, I had a dream. In actuality, I know that it was a personal vision and that my mind was opened. In my vision, I saw myself sitting at a long table. There was a white mist all around, but the air was clear around where I saw myself seated, and I knew I was looking at myself in the premortal existence. Next to me was a man, and we were both wearing white robes. Between us on the table, we had papers, and I watched as we spoke animatedly to each

---

8    "The Opening and Closing of Doors," *Ensign*, October 1987.
9    Job 38:7.

other. Though I heard no words, I knew this man was explaining to me what it was going to be like to be paralyzed. And I watched as my spirit self exclaimed to him, "Ooohhh, I am soooo excited!"

It doesn't matter if I asked for this trial or if someone else asked me to endure it. It matters only that I *knew* it was going to happen, and I was excited for it. We knew what earthly life would be like, and we knew it would be hard—but we still chose to come. We knew we would have work, bad hair days, flat tires, and frustrations, and we were still so excited for those "bad" days that we shouted for joy!

*Staying Excited*

Even with the knowledge I have of my eternal purpose, I still sometimes find myself wondering what my spirit self was thinking. Sometimes I wonder if we, as spirits, were just a tad overzealous about coming to earth. Knowing how excited I was in the premortal existence makes me consider the fact that maybe I didn't understand the extent of this earthly experience I was signing up for. Did my spirit self really understand how difficult it would be down here? Now that I'm really experiencing mortality, how can I be as excited as I was when I was in heaven? How can I muster a positive attitude? And, even harder, how can I muster an *eternal* attitude?

On this side of the veil, I don't think I would have accepted the trial of being paralyzed if I'd been given the choice. It is very hard. I feel awkward at social events because most people don't want to appear rude, so they try not to look at me, and I end up being ignored. I can tell my wheelchair makes people uncomfortable. Sometimes I just want to cry because I wish I could wrap presents as cutely as other people do, but my hands won't work well enough to tie cute bows. It is hard to be me sometimes.

But as hard as it is to be me, it is not any harder than it is to be you.

You don't have to be in a *wheelchair* to know what it feels like when you can't be as fast or as good or as cute as somebody else. You don't have to be in a wheelchair to feel socially awkward. You don't have to be in a wheelchair to know what trials feel like. We all have them. We all travel a rocky path.

And our rocky paths must be traveled with courage. President Gordon B. Hinckley counseled us to have faith when facing our hardships. He said, "Frequently it is not easy to face up to that which is expected of us. Many think they cannot do it. We need a little more faith. We should know that the Lord will not give us commandments beyond our power to observe. He will not ask us to do things for which we lack the capacity. Our problem lies in our fears."[10]

It is easy to be afraid when we have so many challenges, but as difficult and unappealing as our trials are in this life, as we keep our hearts focused on an eternal attitude and remember we are children of our Heavenly Father who loves us, we will be strengthened and brave.

We are all familiar with the plan of salvation, the plan of happiness, or just the plan. Since Primary, we've seen the circles drawn on the chalkboard, which represent the premortal existence, earth life, outer darkness, and the three kingdoms of glory. We've seen various clip art images on the computer. We know what it is.

But here on earth, in the second circle, it seems a little difficult to remember where we came from and where we're going. When we travel down a particularly steep or bumpy part of our path, it's hard to remember whose children we really are so we can say with conviction, "We are sons and daughters of our Heavenly Father, who loves us."

People often ask me if I am always happy or if I sometimes have bad days. The answer is that I rarely struggle with being paralyzed, but, just like anyone else, I have bad, sad, hard *times*.

One such time, which was worse than any time I had encountered prior, happened after I had been paralyzed for a little over six years. I have very vivid dreams, and I awoke from a dream where there were a lot of people Latin dancing. Before being in a wheelchair, I often Latin danced. It was my favorite activity in the whole world. Normally, a dancing dream wouldn't bother me; however, in this particular dream, the other people wouldn't let me

---

10   "Let Us Move This Work Forward," *Ensign*, November 1985.

dance with them. I asked everyone, and they all said no. Waking up to my reality, where I still couldn't dance, was crushing.

I tried to go about my day and do my work, but I couldn't. My heart was too overwhelmed, and I broke down in heavy sobs. I would cry hard for a few minutes, shake it off and dry my eyes, and then burst with another attack of sobs. I couldn't seem to get control of my emotions.

Doubled over in despair and unable to even lift myself back into a sitting position, I remembered hearing that the Savior's Atonement could relieve us of our burdens as well as take away our sins. Emotionally and physically, I couldn't handle this extreme trial; it was crippling me. Calling on the Savior aloud, I begged Him to take it away.

Through my sobs, I thanked Him for letting me feel that pain so deeply. I asked Him to always let me remember the severity of it. I told Him I had faith in His Atonement, and I didn't know if this was the type of pain He could take, but if it was, I asked Him to please take it.

In the very moment I asked, my pain was gone. I stopped crying. I stayed doubled over in my chair and let my arms relax to the floor. My eyes were puffy, and strands of hair were stuck to my wet face, but I smiled in relief, and my heart sang as I felt the Spirit.

It was much the same for the people who followed Alma. They were in bondage to wicked oppressors. They prayed for relief, and the Lord told them He would deliver them eventually, but in the meantime, He said, "[I will ease your burdens] . . . that even you cannot feel them upon your backs, even while you are in bondage; and this will I do that ye may stand as witnesses . . . that I, the Lord God, do visit my people in their afflictions."[11]

The adversary would have loved to see me wallow in my sadness, each sob bringing me closer to spiritual paralysis. Satan doesn't care that I can't dance; he only cares that *I* care about it. Elder Dallin H. Oaks teaches that Christ's Atonement reaches and is powerful enough

---

11　Mosiah 24:14.

not only to pay the price for sin but also to heal every mortal affliction, every heartache and sadness.[12] This experience and others like it have increased my testimony that the Lord does visit His people in their afflictions, and we don't have to feel them. For me, this is the case. I have trials that I can't ignore, but because of my Savior, I rarely feel them.

I know the Savior died for me, and He lives to help me through my mortal life. I am not as strong as He is, but with Him, I can overcome my own trials. Just as He helped the people who followed Alma, I know He will help me. Like the people of Alma, I am strengthened so I can "bear up [my] burdens with ease."[13]

The Savior commanded that we should "be of good cheer" because He has "overcome the world."[14] Though we will have many afflictions, if we seek the Savior's help, strength, and support, through His Atonement, He will come to our aid.

I remember going with my husband to one of his performances at a Hispanic culture fair. At the time, he was my boyfriend, and he played the guitar in a Brazilian style called Bossa Nova. At the event, I sat at our table and enjoyed all the musicians playing their different styles of music from all of the Hispanic countries. After my husband's group performed, he joined me at our table, where we ate beans and rice as we continued to listen to the bands play.

I was surprised when the music changed from live, acoustic music to a recorded heavy rhythmic beat. I looked to the stage to see two Latin dancers start dancing.

My heart started to sink as I felt the vibrations of the music through my wheelchair. This was the very first time I had seen Latin dancers or even heard Latin dancing music since I had been paralyzed. My eyes unexpectedly welled up with tears, and I didn't dare blink or the tears would fall and everyone would know I was crying. I didn't want anyone to feel sad for me, but I knew the tears would eventually fall, so I excused myself from the table and

---

12  "He Heals the Heavy Laden," *Liahona*, November 2006.
13  Mosiah 24:15.
14  John 16:33.

went into the hallway. I rolled behind a large plant and hid. And then I cried.

As I cried, I prayed. I told Heavenly Father I was sorry I was so weak. I tried to be strong, but I didn't always know how. I told Him I knew this earthly life was temporary and I knew I would walk and dance again. I asked Heavenly Father to increase my faith in the plan of salvation.

I stopped crying immediately. My heavy heart lightened, and I could feel the Savior's presence testifying that the plan of salvation was true. I lived in heaven before I came to earth. I will be resurrected. I will stand. And I will dance.

Just then, my husband came out and found me, and we went back in to the event together, where I not only watched the dancers perform, but I also enjoyed it! I was happy for them, and I was happy for me. I was blessed with increased faith in the plan of salvation, and my faith enabled me to enjoy the body I have now and all its limitations.

Satan and his cronies like to point out the sharpest rocks on our trail, remind us how difficult we have it in that one spot and how hard that makes life in general. But as we keep an eternal perspective—remembering who we are, why we're here, where we're going, and just whose children we are—we realize how minor those sharp rocks are, and every time we do, we squish Satan and all his lies between the gaps.

# PRAYER

SATAN'S LAIR SURROUNDS THE PATH we travel each day. He and his followers watch us and strategically plan how they can catch us in a snare to drag us down to spiritual paralysis. It is a war, and we are outnumbered.

This is why the third step to closing our gaps is prayer. Satan's attempts to spiritually paralyze us are real, and we must fight the battle for spiritual ability daily. We will be victorious if we follow the Savior's command to "pray always, that you may come off conqueror; yea, that you may conquer Satan, and that you may escape the hands of the servants of Satan that do uphold his work."[15] If we always have a prayer in our hearts or on our lips, we will be *conquerors* in our daily fights against Satan.

Satan's job is full time, and as strong and as righteous as we are, alone, we are no match for him. If Satan can handicap us spiritually, we're useful to him in paralyzing others through our example because, unlike a physical spinal cord injury, spiritual paralysis is contagious. And unlike being in a wheelchair, spiritual paralysis can be perceived as desirable. Those who are spiritually paralyzed can supposedly do, think, feel, and be whatever they want—they can complain, be lazy, commit sins, and omit righteous doings, all while trying to rest themselves in the gap, away from their rocky path.

But their attempts to hide from their duties and challenges are never successful; there is no rest for them. The only rest available

---

15  D&C 10:5.

in this life is through the Savior. Even in our most challenging times, He has promised us peace. Jesus Christ said, "Peace I leave with you, my peace I give unto you: not as the world giveth, give I unto you."[16] The rest we crave in this life—from our work, pains, frustrations, and sorrows—isn't found in the gaps but rather right on our path.

Prayer is a cry for help and extra strength as we battle the creepy hands of the servants of Satan that reach up from the ravines to try to pull us down with their lies and discouragement. And even though we are absolutely no match for these evildoers, our army of one can be strengthened to include more than just us as lone soldiers. In our fight against Satan's masses, we can pray and then stand with the angels of God, who are just waiting for us to summon their help. They will rush to our aid, and we will be victorious.

Prayer is our secret weapon. We pray in the morning, at mealtime, at night, and whenever we want to or need to. As we pray, we will become the conqueror as the Savior sends us what we need to thwart Satan's attacks. Prayer will give us victory.

We must not rely on prayer alone, though, when it comes to conquering Satan and his tempting whispers each day. We must also follow this old advice: Pray as though everything depends upon God. Work as though everything depends upon you.

Once I was invited to speak at a Rotary Club almost two hours away from my house. They met at seven o'clock in the morning, so to get there on time, I had to leave my house at five. After my presentation and the long drive home, it was still morning. I got out of my car, pulled the heavy laptop bag out of the backseat, and piled it on my lap, along with my purse.

I had recently changed my wheelchair wheels from the battery-powered wheels that magnified my every pushing effort and made my wheelchair very easy to push to regular wheels without any power at all. I wanted to build up strength, and this was a great way to do it—pushing a regular manual wheelchair is hard. I had

---

16 John 14:27.

been using these non-powered wheels for less than a week. I had not yet built up enough strength in my arms to be good at the task. I was slow on regular, flat, smooth ground and even slower on carpet. I couldn't push my wheelchair through the grass at all. I wasn't even able to pop a wheelie.

My husband was at work when I got home from the speaking appointment, and I dreaded coming home to an empty house—not because I didn't want to be alone, but because I didn't think I could get in if there was no one there to help me. The only wheelchair accessible entrance to my house was up a ramp that started at the driveway and led to our front porch and front door. The ramp was a normal, code-approved ramp, but there was a very slanted and steep six-inch piece of wood that connected the ramp to the driveway. This steep, short piece of wood was about a half-inch thick, and I had to first pop a wheelie to get my front wheels onto it and then lean forward and push with all my might, causing my wheelchair to tip upward toward the sky until the ramp leveled out to a decent angle that I could easily roll up. I had successfully pushed myself up this tiny part of the ramp only one time since I had put on the regular, non-powered wheelchair wheels—and that was with a little help.

I approached the ramp, and I frowned and sighed, my breath steaming in the cool morning air. I was so tired. I had just given a presentation, which, by itself, wears me out, but I had also gotten up at four o'clock and driven for over four hours. I knew a nap was only a few feet away in my comfortable, warm house, and I eyed the ramp with determination. I knew I could do it.

I backed up to the edge of my driveway and straightened my chair so I faced the ramp head-on. With a deep breath, I put my hands on the wheels and pushed as quickly as I could to get a "running" start. I soared across the driveway and tried to pop a wheelie over the inch lip of the ramp, but I was going too quickly. I came to an abrupt halt when my front little wheels hit the edge of the ramp, almost throwing my bags off my lap.

I knew speed wouldn't get me over the half-inch lip, and I needed to lift my front wheels over the rise, but popping a wheelie *while* moving forward was beyond my abilities. I could barely do one while I was still.

I faced the ramp again and leaned back while pushing my wheels forward slightly, lifting the front wheels off the driveway and onto the wood. It was the best wheelie I could muster. Without any momentum to help me, I would have to push myself—my wheelchair plus all my little body's dead weight—up the six inches of steep connecting wood and onto the ramp itself. I wiped my tired eyes and put my hands on the wheels. I nodded my head, letting myself know I could do this. I held my breath and began to push with all my might, slowly rolling the little front wheels up the steep wood, but just before the front wheels had made it onto the more level part of the ramp, my big back wheels came onto the steep incline. My whole wheelchair on the sharp angle was too much for me. My hand slipped, and instead of traveling forward and up, I moved backwards and down. I just couldn't get my big wheels up the steep incline.

I was getting cold, and my eyes welled with tears. I just wanted to get inside my house. But crying wasn't going to make the ramp any less steep, so I wiped my tears away and moved around the ramp and toward the porch. I couldn't get myself onto the porch without using the ramp, but I could reach the porch, and I unloaded my laptop and purse there. I was determined to get into my house, and I needed an empty lap and a lighter load to make it up the ramp.

I tried again, this time with an empty lap and renewed determination. I stared at the ramp through the tear residue and pointed at it with my floppy hand. "I own you," I said under my breath. I popped a wheelie and pushed with all my might—only to once again roll back down into the driveway.

I tried a third, fourth, and fifth time, each time getting further and further away from my goal as I got more and more tired.

With cold hands and a runny nose, I looked around my neighborhood. It was a cold morning, and the dark, cloudy sky forecasted gloom. No one was outside. No neighbor was checking his mail, getting his garbage can, or sweeping his porch. And there I sat, in the middle of my driveway, sniffling and alone.

I folded my arms and bowed my head—right there in the driveway—and said a small prayer. In it, I told Heavenly Father what I knew He already knew—that I was tired. That I was cold. That I had gotten up early that morning. That my wheelchair ramp was steep. I told Him that someday soon I would be stronger and be able to make it up the ramp myself, but today I was too weak. I asked Him if He would please send somebody to push me up the ramp.

I know Heavenly Father cares about our most basic needs. I know He hears our prayers. And I knew He would answer mine.

I opened my eyes and looked around hopefully. I just knew the Lord would inspire someone to step out of their house so I could call to them or that a car would drive by and the driver would offer to help. But as I looked, I was disappointed. There was no one at all—just the same lonely neighborhood as before.

I was a little sad. I thought for sure God would send someone. But though my arms were weak, my faith was strong. After all, the Lord will only bless us with what we *need* and not with something we can do for ourselves. Perhaps I really could get up the ramp myself.

With renewed courage, I bumped my little wheels against the edge of the wood and popped a small wheelie. With all my strength, I pushed my wheels up the ramp. My front wheels made it past the steep six-inch incline and onto the level ramp, but the back wheels were so heavy as I labored to push them upward! I couldn't even breathe, but I kept trying.

Every half inch was a mini victory, and I was moments away from getting the back wheels onto the level ramp. As I approached the connection, I teetered on the sharp corner between the steep wood piece and the level ramp. I held my wheels at the corner, just barely below the level ramp, and I tried to nod my head to jerk my chair up and over the corner, but it didn't work. My grip was weakening.

I had pushed with everything I had. I had made it farther than I had ever come before, and when I teetered between the steep and the level—when I had nothing else to give—someone came up behind me, grabbed my wheelchair handles, and gave a push, just enough to make it over the corner and onto the level ramp.

With all four of my wheels on the level ramp, I was able to slowly push myself all the way to the porch. I turned around to see who had given me a push, but no one was there. That is, no one was there who I could see with my mortal eyes. The Lord had heard my prayer and sent someone to push me up the ramp—over the only part I could not do myself.

I smiled as I picked up my bags and went inside.

We sometimes each need a little push over those steep inclines in life, whether they are difficult tests, a rocky relationship, or a lingering illness. But the Lord will not send someone to help us unless we are doing all we can do first.

The Lord blessed Joseph Smith with "sufficient strength"[17] to translate the Book of Mormon, and likewise, we are blessed sufficiently to do the work and endure the trials He gives us.

As we pray and ask, the Lord will bless us with sufficient strength to withstand Satan's followers who continue daily to pull us off the path and spiritually paralyze us. But when we find our grip on righteousness or faith or energy slipping, sincere prayer will summon divine help that will strengthen us.

When we pray sincerely for strength, we will always be heard. The Savior is waiting with blessings to give—but He won't force them on us. He waits until we ask. But just as we would kindly request a favor from a close friend, we must always be kind and loving in our prayers.

There is a proper way to pray. We cannot take our communication with God lightly. We must make our prayers meaningful and pray, as the prophet Moroni said, "with all the energy of heart."[18] As we pray with sincerity, not repetition, we will better hear the Lord when He responds.

A few months after I was paralyzed, I began dating again. One of my dates, who later became my husband, took me to a fireside for a small Sunday night date. I had recently come home from

---

17   D&C 9:12.
18   Moroni 7:48.

the hospital and was feeling self-conscious about my little, lifeless body. My confidence was rock bottom, and it compounded the insecurities we all feel while dating.

Just before the fireside began, a cute girl walked past us to a seat on a pew closer to the front, and I swear my future husband checked her out! He noticed her come in and followed her as she walked to a seat. I watched the whole thing! I was heartbroken and angry. I was embarrassed. I wanted to leave. I was a grumpy date for the rest of the evening, and I insisted he take me home immediately after the fireside.

In my wonderful husband's defense, everyone in the entire congregation had probably been watching her—she had come in late—but at the time, I felt as if there were no excuses. I truly felt wronged. After the date, at home in bed, I lay on my side and sobbed for hours. I was crushed and embarrassed and heartbroken—how could anyone ever see past my disability and love me? How could I ever compete with cute girls with normal bodies? I had so many questions, very much like the ones I know everyone has, regardless of their abilities. Being self-conscious is a universal feeling, one with which everyone is painfully familiar.

On one of the rockiest parts of my path and in the depth of my anger and self-pity, I turned to prayer. I insisted that the Lord hear me. I told Him what had happened and asked Him to give me peace and comfort. I asked for Him to calm my troubled heart. I told Him to take the pain away.

But as I asked for these things, which in my opinion were very small things to ask for, I felt nothing. I prayed again, repeating my words over and over, begging for the Lord to hear me and bless me with peace and solace and comfort.

Nothing.

I cried hard and prayed harder. *Please calm my troubled heart! I need peace. Please give me peace. Isn't that what You do?! I am so upset. Why aren't You hearing me? I know You can do this. Why are You withholding Your blessings from me?*

As I prayed, I got more upset. I was not receiving the peace I felt I needed. I felt I was being ignored. I knew the Lord could hear me—I have a testimony that He hears all prayers—but for some reason, He was refusing to answer me.

In the midst of a deep sob, it dawned on me that Heavenly Father *was* trying to answer my prayer, but I was not allowing Him to. I was pouring out my heart to Him, but that was all—I wasn't allowing myself to listen to what He was trying to tell me. I was too angry and too distressed to let Him bless me with the peace I needed.

I realized my mistake. I needed to calm down and hear and feel Heavenly Father's answer. But I was emotionally charged, hurt, embarrassed, and angry. I was also tired. In my weak and bruised voice, I repented. I told Heavenly Father I was sorry. I knew He answered prayers and that He was trying to answer mine, but I was not letting Him. I asked for forgiveness. I told Heavenly Father how upset I was. I told Him how tired I was. I knew everything would be better in the morning, and I said, "Please, just put me to sleep."

President Thomas S. Monson said that when a child prays to God, God listens.[19] Aren't we all Heavenly Father's children? Once I had spoken those words, *just put me to sleep*, I immediately stopped crying. My arms relaxed on the bed. My shoulders relaxed. My head and neck relaxed. My eyes closed, and I fell asleep until morning.

Heavenly Father answers prayers. He answers mine, and He answers yours. He waits for us to come to Him—praying is part of our agency, and we have the choice to do it or not. He waits for us to use our agency to call to Him. When we do call out in prayer, He will come running with the blessings we need.

Humble prayer is a powerful tool for keeping Satan at bay, and we know that we should pray always—when we get up, when we go to bed, and all the time in between. The Savior commanded us to do everything in His name, whether it's a sacrament meeting or a barbecue prayer. It will help us center our daily activities on the Savior.

One daily activity that should include prayer is scripture study. As Latter-day Saints, we have been taught all our lives to make prayer

---

19 "Come Listen to a Prophet's Voice: Pray Always," *Friend*, July 2001.

a part of our scripture study so it can help us humbly read the verses, understand them, and apply meanings. But let me ask you this: have you ever considered making scripture study a part of your prayer?

Elder Robert D. Hales said it best when he counseled us to turn to our scriptures to hear the voice of the Lord. He said, "When we want to speak to God, we pray. And when we want Him to speak to us, we search the scriptures."[20] Making scripture study a part of prayer will turn our one-sided prayer into a conversation with the Lord. We pray and tell the Lord everything we have in our hearts—what we're thinking, needing, wanting, doing—and as we read the scriptures, Heavenly Father answers us sincerely.

Heavenly Father speaks through His scriptures. They were written for us to read today, and they contain God's words, not just a giant grouping of irrelevant information written many years ago. They are specific words with an application for each of us. When we read from the pages of the ancient scriptures, we hear Heavenly Father speak to us through the Holy Ghost to answer our current questions, address our current concerns, and calm us in our current daily battles.

We will be strengthened to fight our battles as we read the scriptures. There is no limit to the personal insights they can provide as we include them in our prayers. There is no such feeling or insight when I read a novel or look at a cookbook; I feel that unique, heart-hugging, soul-smile only when I read from the pages of the Book of Mormon and other scriptures. President Henry B. Eyring promised that if we read the Book of Mormon with an open heart, we will know it is the true word of God, and we will feel its power to change our lives for the better.[21]

President Spencer W. Kimball told the members of the Church that he was "convinced that each of us, at some time in our lives, must discover the scriptures for ourselves."[22] He wants

---

20  "Holy Scriptures: The Power of God unto Our Salvation," *Ensign*, November 2006.
21  "A Discussion on Scripture Study," *Ensign*, July 2005.
22  "How Rare a Possession—the Scriptures!" *Ensign*, September 1976.

us to discover the scriptures because as we read them after we pray, we have the opportunity to converse with the Savior through the Spirit. This is revelation. Revelation is often talked about, but we have to practice receiving it to understand how it works. After we pray, we may find that the scripture chapter may or may not be discussing what we have prayed about, but the Spirit can touch our hearts and use the written scriptural words to answer us, thus making our prayers a conversation with the Lord.

In my life, I have received answers from scriptural words and phrases that have had seemingly nothing to do with my question. Once, after dating a boy a few times, I had a very strong impression that I was to pray and ask Heavenly Father if I should continue to date him. My answer came through the scriptures as I read this verse in Third Nephi: "But Gidgiddoni saith unto them: The Lord forbid; for if we should go up against them the Lord would deliver us into their hands; therefore we will prepare ourselves in the center of our lands, and we will gather all our armies together, and we will not go against them, but we will wait till they shall come against us; therefore as the Lord liveth, if we do this he will deliver them into our hands."[23]

These are the words of Gidgiddoni, one of the righteous Nephite army leaders. The Nephites had asked Gidgiddoni to lead them in an attack against the Gadianton robbers, and they wanted to battle on the Gadianton robbers' own land. This verse is Gidgiddoni's reply to them: the Lord forbids it.

This verse isn't about dating. This verse isn't about boyfriends or even friend-friends. This verse is about nothing seemingly relevant to my life, but it answered my question as to whether or not I should date the boy I had been seeing.

As I read the words *the Lord forbid*, my heart burned and the Spirit's presence was strong. Nothing else from that scripture stuck out to me the way those three words did: *the Lord forbid*.

Nowhere in the scriptures did any of the ancient prophets write about cell phones, borrowing clothes, rude school friends,

---

23  3 Nephi 3:21.

or university classes, but these are just some of the things I have received answers about through the scriptures.

As a youth, the Prophet Joseph Smith had a great question weighing on his mind: which church he should join? He started reading the Bible and found guidance in the book of James (see James 1:5). He said, "Never did any passage of scripture come with more power to the heart of man than this did at this time to mine."[24] He reflected on it "again and again." Because Joseph acted on what he read in the scriptures, he learned about Heavenly Father, His Son Jesus Christ, the Holy Ghost, and his identity as a son of God. Joseph learned who he was, why he was here on earth, and what he needed to do in this life.

No matter how complicated and not ancient my question is, I know Heavenly Father can and will guide me to my answer through the scriptures, both ancient and modern. President Dieter F. Uchtdorf said that reading the words of the prophet will guide us to our beautiful and eternal destination—at the end of our path![25] Scripture prophets are important, but President Ezra Taft Benson counseled us on the importance of modern prophets as well. He said, "The living prophet is more vital to us than the standard works."[26] We must study modern prophets as much as we study ancient prophets, and as we read different verses from the scriptures or articles from the *Ensign* or *Liahona*, the Spirit will act as an interpreter and burn in our hearts, and we will know the Lord is speaking to us.

Even when we don't have any pressing issues in our lives, we must follow the counsel President Eyring gave when he explained that he reads the scriptures while asking himself, "What would God have me do?"[27]

Recently, as I began my day with a conversation with my Heavenly Father—praying and reading the scriptures—He told me to clean my house.

---

24  JS—H 1:12.
25  "Your Happily Ever After," *Ensign*, May 2010.
26  "Fourteen Fundamentals in Following the Prophet," in *Speeches of the Year, 1980* [Provo: Brigham Young University, 1981], 26.
27  "A Discussion on Scripture Study."

What? I thought this counsel was bizarre and unnecessary. It was frustrating advice too, because I had a lot to accomplish, including getting an important check out to the mailbox before the mailman came that morning. I felt I needed to get to work, but the scriptures were clearly telling me, for some reason, that Heavenly Father wanted me to clean my house.

So I put aside my lengthy to-do list and started to clean. I made my bed, loaded some clothes in the washing machine, tidied up the kitchen, swept the floors, and picked up the living room. I even wiped down the walls. In my very last effort to clean my house, I straightened the couch. It was off center just a few inches. As I did, I noticed something under it—my purse.

Had I forsaken the counsel given to me that morning to clean my house and continued on with the very important first item on my to-do list, to put a check in the mail before the mailman came, I would have first looked for my purse, which would have been impossible to find. I would have panicked and called my husband. We would have both torn the house apart looking for it. Because I started my busy day by conversing with my Heavenly Father, I avoided a stressful situation and was still able to accomplish my to-do list.

Plus, I had a clean house.

When I was nineteen, I received a much needed revelation through the scriptures. Before I was married to my wonderful husband and before I was even paralyzed, I was interning at Disney World in Orlando, Florida. While there, I met a cute guy, who was also on an internship, and the two of us fell "madly in love" and were engaged almost immediately.

It was a very exciting, whirlwind relationship. He was excited, all our friends were excited, my parents were excited, and my friends back home were excited. There was only one person who wasn't excited—me.

I was not excited because I knew in my heart that Heavenly Father did not want me to marry him. I was crushed. Devastated. I didn't understand. Everything seemed normal on the outside—he was being righteous and so was I. We were going to get married in the temple. But for reasons I did not understand at the time, Heavenly Father wanted me to break up with him.

Having Heavenly Father say no is the most difficult answer to receive, but it is not binding. Heavenly Father has given us a special gift to use while we are on this earth—our agency. We have the choice to follow His commandments and guidance for us or not to. If we do, we will prosper. If we don't, we will be spiritually paralyzed. It is that simple.

In my case, I didn't want to break up with this guy. I desperately wanted to marry him. I remember being on my knees for hours, begging Heavenly Father to approve, to say yes. I didn't want to do it without His approval, but I wanted it so much. I told Him I'd do anything He ever wanted me to do if He would only let me marry this person. After hours on the floor, I heard Heavenly Father sigh and say okay.

I jumped off my knees and clapped my hands! The moment was short-lived, however, and I dropped back onto my knees again, saying, "I know You didn't mean that."

Even though I knew Heavenly Father's answer was no, I continued to ask Him anyway, hoping it would change. In that hope, I stopped asking that particular question ("Should I marry this guy?") and instead changed it to a different question: *Should I move to Massachusetts when my internship ends?* As the days went by and our internships were coming to a close, we discussed the idea of me moving to his home state of Massachusetts to get a job, find an apartment near his home, and finish going to school.

I was hoping that when Heavenly Father said no to my request to get married, He had really just meant "not right now" and that maybe, just maybe, I could move to Massachusetts and continue to date this guy so we could get married later. I will save you the anticipation of wondering if this was the case. It wasn't and never will be. When Heavenly Father says no, He means no, and if He wants to say "later," then that's what He'll say.

But in my youthful foolishness, I continued asking for a couple of weeks, and my answer came on a windy Sunday afternoon. After church, I found a nice shady spot under a tree, where I could sit at an outside picnic table. I tossed my scriptures on the table and as I did so, they landed open. I sat down and folded my arms to pray first and also ask the same question I had been asking: *Should I move to Massachusetts and get a job and an apartment and start going to school? Maybe this just isn't the right time for us to be married, but maybe in a few months, the answer will be different. Maybe he should move to Utah—would that work, Heavenly Father? Or should I just go home to Utah while he goes home to Massachusetts?*

As I prayed, the wind blew my scripture pages, and they opened to a page that was in between bookmarks. (You know how it is easier to turn to a page in your scriptures that already has a bookmark but more difficult to turn in between already marked pages? Enough said.)

I opened my eyes and smiled—I just knew the breeze had blown my scripture pages to the page with the answer to my question! I looked down and read the first verse I saw: *"Every man turn to his own people, and flee every one into his own land."*[28]

*Um. This can't be right,* I thought. I stared at the verse for a few moments. *Hmm. Every man to his own land?* I wondered if that meant I should go to Utah and he should go to Massachusetts. I wondered if that was my answer. I did not want that answer. I really did not want that answer. I totally, definitely, absolutely did not want that answer.

As we often do when we receive revelation that we don't want, I dismissed it. I turned in my scriptures to where I was reading in Second Nephi. But before I started reading the first verse of the chapter, my eyes wandered to the left side of the page, where I read this scripture: *"Every man turn to his own people, and flee every one into his own land."*[29]

I guess that was my answer.

So I broke up with him. He moved back to Massachusetts, and I moved back to Utah—our own "lands." I gave back my big, beautiful diamond ring and gave up the imagined future I could have had.

---

28   Isaiah 13:14; emphasis added.
29   2 Nephi 23:14; emphasis added.

Breaking off that first engagement was the most difficult thing I have ever done. It was harder than being paralyzed, harder than relearning how to breathe, harder than rejoining life in a wheelchair. It was the hardest thing I've ever done because I could see no reason for it, and I had the choice *not to*. Because of my agency, I could have chosen to dismiss every revelation that didn't agree with my personal agenda. I could have stepped off my life path and into spiritual paralysis and done everything I wanted. I didn't understand why Heavenly Father was saying no—everything on the outside seemed fine.

Even though breaking off that first engagement was the hardest thing I have ever done—without exception—I would do it again to marry my husband. We got married in February 2008, four years after I was paralyzed. A few days before we went to the Salt Lake Temple to be sealed, I was in my bedroom, sitting next to my bed in my wheelchair. I leaned onto the bed and opened my scriptures. Since I'd become paralyzed, I'd begun marking my pages with a fat, lime-green marker. As I opened the book, I saw all the lime-green markings on the pages, and my mind opened up. I remembered a dream I'd had many years before, when I was engaged in Florida.

In the dream, I'd opened a book and could see lime-green markings. I looked above the pages and saw two men standing in the air. On the left was my then-fiancé in Florida. On the right was a man I did not recognize at the time, but I really wanted to marry him; my heart ached to be with him.

As I relived this dream, this time while I was awake, I looked above my scriptures with the lime-green markings, and the same two men were standing in the air above the bed. The man on the left was my ex-fiancé from Florida. But this time I recognized the man on the right as my husband.

Heavenly Father knows what we want, and He knows what trials, struggles, and blessings will help us get it. When He says no, it isn't because He is trying to be mean or because He is always trying to test our faith. He is helping us get those things in this life that will make us the most happy. But if we refuse to act on the answers He gives us when we pray, we will become spiritually paralyzed.

Even though I receive *most* of my answers to prayer through the scriptures, they aren't the only way to talk with Heavenly Father. I have received answers through quiet pondering, good books, other people, and even commercials. When we are listening, Heavenly Father can speak to us through any means at all. Once, when I needed to choose between two tough choices, I got my answer through a fortune cookie. The key is to have the "interpreter," the Holy Spirit, to confirm that the answer is from Heavenly Father.

But what if our prayer doesn't ask for knowledge? What if we need help—immediate help? What if our path has become too rocky for us to travel on our own? What if we need a *miracle*?

I believe in miracles. I know Heavenly Father is all powerful, and He can do anything. I have been blessed to see some of His miracles performed in my life. But often, our prayers are answered through the good deeds of others. President Kimball said, "God does notice us, and he watches over us. But it is usually through another person that he meets our needs."[30]

I'm reminded of a time when I went with the young women in my ward to do baptisms for the dead. I, along with several other leaders, met the girls in our church parking lot, and the young women divided into our various cars. My car is a four-door Subaru Baja. To drive it, I use hand controls on the steering wheel, and my wheelchair rides in the bed. To get my wheelchair back there, I first slide over to the driver's seat, using a long, wooden slide-board that bridges the gap (no pun intended) between my wheelchair and the driver's seat. Once in the car, I use a remote control to bring a small crane around from the back of my car to my door. Then I use the remote control to lower a cable, and I hook my wheelchair to the cable and use the remote to pick up the chair and set it in the back.

That's it!

Three young women piled into my car, and we were the first group to leave the church parking lot to drive to the Ogden Temple. The other groups were going to wait for more girls to arrive. We

---

30   "Small Acts of Service," *Ensign*, December 1974.

parked on the side of the temple, where there were fewer cars, and the girls got out and stood next to my door. They were excited to watch me get out.

I was feeling pretty cool—after all, I had a cool car with a cool wheelchair lift in the back! I just knew these girls would be so impressed. I picked up the remote and pushed the button to lift the crane (and show off)—but nothing worked.

I pushed the buttons harder and harder, but the crane wasn't moving at all. One of the young women took the remote to see if she could get it to work, but she couldn't. Then the other two young women tried and neither of them could get it to work either. I was frustrated because we were at the *temple*, and I felt like I should be blessed, not punished. Going to the temple should be *easy* not hard.

But I've learned that all our offerings—whether it's serving at the temple or our tithing or our fast—are more meaningful if they are difficult. King David said, "Neither will I offer . . . offerings unto the Lord my God of that which doth cost me nothing."[31] The cost of our offerings can be money, but it can also be time, energy, or strength, and from the ravine, Satan will whisper that the price is too high, you're too tired, and it's too much. . . .

I knew that getting to the temple this day was going to "cost" me more than other days, and Satan's whisperings were hard at work. My crane and remote sometimes had mechanical troubles that were easy fixes for my husband but not for me. Additionally, the young women were not strong enough to lift my heavy wheelchair from the bed of the car, especially because the crane was weighing it down.

An idea came to my mind—this could be a faith-promoting experience for these young women! I sat in the driver's seat with the door open and gathered my three young women closer to me.

I asked them if they believed that God knew where we were and what we were trying to do.

They nodded that He did.

---

31  2 Samuel 24:24.

"Are we being righteous in going to the temple to do baptisms for the dead?"

"Yes!"

"Do you believe God helps people do righteous things?"

"Yes!" They were getting excited.

"Do you think God will hear our prayer and make the crane work so we can all go inside the temple together?"

"Yes, He will! He will!"

Heavenly Father was going to show these girls a miracle! I knew He could fix the crane; I knew it because I'd *seen* Him do it—twice. We huddled in close and bowed our heads. After our short but sincere prayer, we all looked at each other hopefully. The girls were smiling, and I knew they had faith that my crane would work. I picked up the remote control and pushed the button . . . .

It totally didn't work.

I pushed it again and again—but nothing! The crane wouldn't budge. I looked at the young women, and I saw the disappointment on their faces. I was disappointed too and a little confused. I prayed in my heart as I furiously pushed the buttons harder and harder. *Heavenly Father! Why are You withholding Your blessing from us? Don't You see that these young women need this faith-building experience?*

But still, the crane refused to move. I was confused, but I knew the Lord answered prayers, and there was a good reason He was choosing to say no to this one.

I asked my three disappointed young women, "Did God hear our prayer?"

They all nodded, and I bore a short testimony and shared how I know God hears and answers all prayers—even if it isn't in the way we want Him to. I told them there was a good reason the Lord wouldn't make the crane work.

The other leaders were not supposed to be there for a while longer, and we were supposed to be the first group to be baptized. I asked the girls what they wanted to do. I smiled as they promised to be reverent if I would let them go inside without me.

The young women got back into my car, and I drove to the front of the temple and parked in a stall close to the door but next to the small parking lot road leading to the street. I gathered the young women around my door once again and explained to them how to get to the baptismal rooms and what to tell the temple worker when they got there.

Just as they were about to leave, a small car drove slowly by us on the small road heading toward the street. The young man inside was about mission age, maybe recently returned. He drove by us slowly, very slowly. He and I made eye contact, and we stared at each other as he drove. When he was almost past us, I silently nodded my head yes.

As I nodded, I blinked my eyes a few times and scrunched up my face—what was I doing? He immediately turned his car around and came to us. He asked if we needed help.

The young women were delighted to see him, partly because he was cute but mostly because he was strong enough to lift the wheelchair out of the back of the car. They knew God had heard our prayer!

Our prayers are powerful messages to a loving Heavenly Father, who sits waiting to hear from us. When we use our agency to close the gaps by being grateful, keeping an eternal attitude, and praying, Satan and his followers are no match for the army we can summon to our aid. Though they try daily to spiritually paralyze us by whispering that the price of our offering is too high, we will find relief in miraculous ways as angels—heavenly and mortal—watch over us. As we pray, we will be strengthened, warmed, comforted, and given the power to withstand the creeping fingers of the adversary as he unsuccessfully tries to pull us down and spiritually paralyze us.

The bigger lesson for me and those young women to learn was not that Heavenly Father is a God of inexplicable miracles, but that we, as brothers and sisters in this life, answer each other's prayers. This is why the final step in closing the gaps is service. Not only are our prayers answered, but we can also be the answer to others' prayers and help them close their gaps.

# SERVICE

KEEPING SATAN AWAY FROM US and closing the gaps little by little doesn't make the path we walk any softer, but we don't have to feel those rough spots on our soles. There is one more step to closing the gaps that, if taken, will lift us and alleviate the rough, pokey, and sharp sections of our trail. That step is service.

We might ask, "How can service help *me* in *my* journey?" We might wonder how serving could help lighten our load when it would inevitably be heavier if we carried someone else's burdens.

The world tells us that when we're having a hard time, we're supposed to focus on *our* problems. Once *our* path is smooth and *our* lives are easy, then we will have the ability to carry someone else's burden.

There are two things wrong with this thinking. First, think of those you know best. Are their lives perfect and their paths flat? No. There's an old saying that goes, "If someone appears to have no problems, you don't know them very well." Second, try this exercise: Starting right now, don't swallow. Not at all—did you swallow? Don't do it. Is your mouth getting dry? Is your throat feeling the air you breathe? Breathe in . . . breathe out . . . breathe in . . . feel how dry your throat is. Gross. Don't swallow. Don't do it. Three more seconds . . . two . . . one . . .

Okay, swallow. Good job. Did you have a difficult time trying not to swallow? Some people struggle a lot with this exercise, others not so much. I suppose it all depends on when you last had a drink.

We all thirst for something in this life, whether we've been single much longer than all our friends and we're thirsting for a meaningful relationship or we're thirsting for our son or daughter to come back to the gospel. We are all thirsting for something. Though we try our best each day to quench our thirst, at least for a time, we're stuck walking along our difficult path, unable to swallow.

We can never quench our thirst by thinking about how thirsty we are. We can never moisten our throats by thinking about how we can't swallow. So we forge ahead, thirsty for something and having faith that Jesus Christ will quench our thirst with His living water.

Until then, we're stuck being thirsty, and we have to ignore it the best we can. But how can we forget our own thirst? When I was young, I would sometimes get thirsty during sacrament meeting (we weren't ever allowed to leave), and my mom would tell me to *think about something else*. While that counsel didn't really help me much as a six-year-old, I've grown to recognize that it is actually excellent advice.

Refocusing our attention on something else is not only effective, but it also heals us and makes us happy. But in our everyday lives, we have bigger problems than a one-hour thirsty spell, and we need bigger things to focus on. It sounds crazy, I know, but I have found that when I am on a particularly rocky part of the path and thirsty for a smooth patch, the best way to even the terrain and forget my own thirst is to help another person.

When I help someone else, I'm quenching their thirst in any small way I can, and I'm forgetting how thirsty I was to begin with. When others help me, they also forget their own thirst as they help me quench mine. We all need each other to be happy, and not because other people's happiness is our first priority but because ours is. President Uchtdorf counseled us that lasting happiness comes, not from looking to our own needs, but from looking to the needs of others.[32] As we look to the needs of others and help to quench their thirst, our own needs are met and our own thirst forgotten.

Satan would have us believe that we don't have the strength, the energy, or the time to look to the needs of others. He will remind

---

32  "Happiness, Your Heritage," *Ensign*, November 2008.

us of our own thirst. But President Uchtdorf said that looking to the needs of others is where we find happiness—even amid our own rocky paths. As we look to the needs of others, our own troubles fade to the background, and we feel lighter as we carry their burdens, not heavier!

When I graduated from high school, I had one goal—go to Germany. I was an overly obsessed eighteen-year-old, and I couldn't wait to go to Germany to work and attend college.

I did not have the resources to simply travel there, so I chose to become a nanny. With my nanny position, I would have a place to live and people to guide me and teach me more about living in the country. My goal was to be a nanny for one year and then venture out into the country alone and go to a university.

It seemed like a good idea.

But there are personalities well suited to being a nanny, and mine is just not one of them. I lasted only five days until I was kicked out!

I was crushed. Devastated. The whole five days was a culture-shocked blur. I flew home teary-eyed and unable to eat or sleep on the plane. All my dreams were ruined. I had no backup plan.

I didn't know how I would face my boyfriend either. We had been dating for almost a year, and our plan was that I would go live in Germany for a time to learn German, while he would leave for a mission shortly thereafter and (hopefully) learn another language. Then he would return home, and I would return home, and we would get married and have kids who would be tri-lingual.

That was our plan anyway.

As soon as my plane touched down in Utah, I called him in tears and sobs—after all, I'd just been kicked out of a foreign country! But those tears and sobs were nothing compared to what was about to come. My heart, which was already sunk, was crushed as I listened to him tell me that while I'd been gone for those five days, he had found another girlfriend. And he had *kissed* her!

I had been gone only *five* days!

*Five* days!

In just under one week, I had experienced culture shock, disappointment, and true failure. And to top it all off, I had been dumped. I laid on the floor next to my bed in the fetal position and sobbed for three days straight. I cried so hard I would make myself throw up, then I would return to the floor and cry some more. I lost eleven pounds.

Up to that point, I had never been sadder. As I sobbed on the floor, I thought of a friend of mine who had also recently been dumped by her boyfriend. She was angry at him, angry at herself, and angry at God.

Who is easier to blame than God? After all, we've been taught since Primary that God *knows all things*—He knows the beginning from the end, the front from the back, the inside from the out. If He really does know all things, why wouldn't He stop this from happening? Why wouldn't He fix it? Sometimes, in our darkest hours, it feels as if God has forgotten about us. It feels as if He is too busy to care about us in our trials, which is terrible because we *know* that He knows we're enduring them. Jacob taught, "For he knoweth all things, and there is not anything save he knows it."[33] So naturally, God is an appropriate target to blame when things in our life go wrong. Right? After all, He could fix it if He wanted to. Elder David S. Baxter understood this feeling when he said, "God is forsaken in the all-too-human yet mistaken fear that He has forsaken us."[34] Because my friend could not get past her disappointments, she left the Church, blaming God for the massive frustrations in her life.

While I lay on the floor crying, I thought of how easy it would be for me to blame God. *Why was He letting this happen to me? Didn't He care? Why did He let me get kicked out of Germany? Didn't He know how badly I wanted to be there? Why had He let my boyfriend dump me? What had I done to deserve this? Nothing!*

I thought again of my friend who had left the Church because her life had severe challenges.

---

33 2 Nephi 9:20.
34 "Faith, Service, Constancy," *Ensign*, November 2006.

And I decided I did not want to do that.

But I didn't know *what* to do. So, wet with tears and smelling like vomit, I mustered the very best prayer I could and repeated it over and over through my sobs. *Please don't let me blame this on the Church. Please don't let me blame this on the Church. Please don't let me blame this on the Church . . . .*

I went to church that next Sunday. I was embarrassed because I had to explain to everyone why I was home and relive all the heartbreaking details of my failed attempt to live in Germany. All the while, my heart was wrenching as I thought of my ex-boyfriend and his new girlfriend. It seemed that *every* guy in my ward reminded me of him.

The Relief Society president, however, did not seem very sympathetic to my obvious sadness and asked me (since I was still going to be home) if I would like to be the chorister in Relief Society. "Sure," I told her. "I guess."

I went to Sunday School, and the bishop pulled me aside afterward to tell me they had not yet released me from my calling as the ward young single adult representative. He asked me (since I was still going to be home) if I would continue to serve in that calling. "Sure," I said. "I guess."

After sacrament meeting, the bishop caught me again and pulled me into his office to ask me (since I was still going to be home) if I would direct the ward road show. I was kind of excited about that one.

After church, the stake president called me into his office and asked me (since I was still going to be home) if I would be the young single adult president for the stake.

Whoa.

When I got home from church that day, I had four callings and a testimony that when I am sad, Heavenly Father wants me—and all of us—to serve. He had heard my feeble but sincere prayer, and He was helping me get through that rough patch of trail.

As I served in those four callings over the next few months, I was focused on others and their needs, not my own. Somehow, not focusing on myself and what I thought I needed gave me exactly what I did need—opportunities to forget how thirsty I was for my old boyfriend and for Germany. While I was focused on others, Heavenly Father was focused on me.

As we serve others, Heavenly Father will help us smooth our path so we won't feel the sharp rocks. He won't always remove them; He waits for us to smooth them out ourselves through service. Experiencing the power of service has healed my heart and smoothed my path many times.

After I was paralyzed and then released from the hospital, my path became more rocky and troublesome than it had ever been before. Everything was different and difficult. One of the hardest things was that I couldn't control my body temperature, so I was often too cold or too hot. I was released from the hospital in June, and I spent my days outside on the back porch in the warm summer sun.

I preferred to be outside because the sunshine and breezes felt good, but I didn't feel good. All I would do, day after day, was sit on the back porch and watch the grass grow. I would just sit there— like a lump. It was a horrible feeling. I wish I were exaggerating, but I'm not. Every day—all day—I sat there doing nothing.

Occasionally, friends would stop by to visit for a short time, but no one ever stayed long. I don't blame them; I was grumpy and thirsty for the "old me." My parents were stressed, and my brothers and sister had other things to do. I was useless—a lump of nothing. I couldn't work at my old job. I was not in school. I didn't go on dates. I couldn't even cut my own meat, let alone feed myself.

As I sat there on the porch one day, I remembered hearing someone from the hospital say that no work is the hardest work of all because we can't stop to rest. I thought about how true that was.

I remembered the life lesson on service I'd received a few years earlier when I was kicked out of Germany and dumped. I realized that the only person who could quench my thirst was my Savior, the Living Water. If I was ever to quench this thirst and soften this rough patch, I needed to serve.

I asked my mom to push me down the street to a nearby elementary school. She pushed me to the main office, where I asked the principal, Mrs. Frodsham, if there was anything I could do to help. Mrs. Frodsham was very kind and took pity on me. She assigned me to help in Mrs. Smith's second grade class.

I sat outside the door in the hallway, and one at a time, students came out to sit in a tiny chair next to me and read me their library books. I would just sit there and encourage the students, saying things like, "Good job," "Good reading," "That's wonderful," "That's a good book," and "I'm glad you picked that one." That was really all I would do; I was just a cheerleader. I had a clipboard on my lap with a list of all the students, and when they were done, I would have them take the pencil and put a check mark next to their own name. I couldn't do it myself because, at that time, I didn't know how to use a pencil. After they had checked off their own name, they called for the next student because I was too weak to speak that loudly.

And that was it.

That was all I did.

I am not dumb. If you look at what I was doing, with the clipboard on my lap, I could have been replaced by a desk. Some people might think my service there was small, inconsequential, and seemingly meaningless.

But it was none of those things to me.

Albert Einstein once said that a person starts to live when he can live outside himself, and that is exactly what happened to me. Through that small but deliberate act of service, a whole new world opened to me. Soon after I started volunteering at that elementary school, I began to feel alive again. Though my path was very rocky, I was starting to feel the burden of my trial lessen. I was happier.

After a few months, I joined the Utah Wheelchair Rugby Team, the Scorpions. I went back to school. I heard about the national Ms. Wheelchair America pageant and went to represent Utah. I won the spirit award.

As President Hinckley said, "Work will cure your grief. Serve others."[35] Work certainly cured my grief as I served others. As I forgot myself, the Lord "remembered" me. As I carried the burdens of others,

---

35  Dieter F. Uchtdorf, "Happiness, Your Heritage," *Ensign*, November 2008.

the Lord carried me. There was a magazine article written about me. They interviewed Brad Zollinger, who is the rehabilitation director for the hospital where I was recovering. He said, "Meg has made one of the most remarkable recoveries of any patient we have had the opportunity to serve."[36] I attribute that entire recovery to the small service I provided those second graders.

My small service at the elementary school was just that—small. It was small but deliberate. Mother Teresa said, "If you can't feed a hundred people, then feed just one."[37] The mouth I ended up feeding was my own. As I continued to serve, I started to feel really good about what I was doing. I thought, *You know, a desk couldn't encourage these kids—maybe I'm better than a desk. Maybe I'm not just a lump of nothing.*

President Spencer W. Kimball said, "So often our acts of service consist of simple encouragement or of giving mundane help with mundane tasks—but what glorious consequences can flow from mundane acts and from small but deliberate deeds."[38] I know the truth of President Kimball's words; I have felt the "glorious consequences" that have resulted from that and other small acts of service.

The hospital fixed me, but serving healed me. President Uchtdorf promised that heaven will pour down choice blessings if we will just serve.[39]

Service smooths our path and strengthens us in ways that we can't do ourselves. When Satan reminds us of our trials and hardships and points out sharp rocks on our path, he is trying to get us to focus on ourselves. He wants us to think we don't have enough resources to even manage ourselves, let alone serve someone else. Life is hard on everyone—everyone. Sometimes the storms of life beat down so heavily that we think there is no sunshine anywhere

36  Allison Hansen, "Embracing Change," *Wasatch Woman Magazine,* January/February 2008.
37  http://www.searchquotes.com/quotation/If_you_can't_feed_a_hundred_people,_then_just_feed_one./227905/
38  "There Is Purpose in Life," *New Era,* September 1974.
39  "Happiness, Your Heritage."

in sight. In the storms of life, we may wonder if we can even be useful to another person—*we* may be the ones needing help out of the storm.

Sometimes these storms are figurative, and sometimes they are literal. When I got married in 2008, I took up genealogy (because that's what married people do, right?). One day I went to the genealogy library to do some research. It had been raining hard all day long. I'd lived in Utah for many years, and I'd never seen it rain so hard before. When I was done at the library, I pushed my wheelchair through the rain to my car. Because of the downpour, my hands kept slipping, and the raindrops beat down on my neck. My hair was soaked.

I opened my car door and wedged my wheelchair as close as I could. But when I tried to slide my bum into the car, it didn't go.

The rain was so heavy that it had soaked the wooden slide-board, which now stuck to my jeans. So the slide-board was stuck to my bum, and when I tried to push myself into the car, I "grabbed" the slide-board with my tush and threw it into the car . . . without me.

The push off my wheelchair sent it rolling down into the parking lot . . . without me.

I went straight down on the ground—into a water puddle!

I couldn't believe it. There I was, sitting *next* to my car, in a *water puddle*—in the *rain*.

I was wet. I was cold. I was mad.

*Heavenly Father!* I cried in my heart as I furrowed my brows and looked up into the pouring rain. *I was doing genealogy—for YOU!*

I wanted to call my husband, but I couldn't. The first thing I do in a car transfer is throw my purse (with my phone) into the passenger seat.

Awesome.

There I sat, looking pathetic and feeling even worse. Genealogy is kind of an old person "sport," so I knew that anyone I saw (if I saw anyone) was going to be old. The only thing I could do was wait for someone to come by so I could ask them to hand me my phone. That way I could call my husband to come help me.

As I waited, a big white van without windows drove slowly toward me. You know, one of those kidnapper vans? I fluffed my hair and tried to look natural. *Doo doo doo,* I hummed. *This is where I mean to be . . . on the ground, in a puddle, in a rainstorm.* He didn't even stop! And again, I was left alone, wondering how I was ever going to get back in the car.

Just then, a little old lady peered around the car door. With a sweet voice that could only belong to a grandmother, she looked down at me and said, "I know you're probably okay, but I was just wondering if there was something I could do."

Embarrassed but relieved, I smiled up at her through the rain. "Yes," I said. "I've fallen, and I can't get back into my car. My husband works really close. Could you hand me my phone so I can call him?"

Her wrinkled eyes flashed into a deep smile as she peered down at me. She tilted her head and gave me a look that only the wise can give, as if to prepare me for a lesson only she could teach. "Oh, no," she said, shaking her head. Then she nodded encouragingly. "I think we can do it."

In disbelief, I stared up at her. She was maybe one hundred pounds—but only because her rain-soaked clothes added a few pounds. She was skinny and old and frail.

She shuffled closer to me and reached out for my hand.

I part laughed, part cried in irritation. As politely as I could, I tried to say, "No, thank you; I really don't think—"

"Oh, yes," she interrupted, "I think we can." She came closer.

My eyes widened in surprise then furrowed in confusion. "No, no," I said, shaking my head. "I'm too heavy!"

Unhearing, she reached down and picked up my left arm with both her hands. "I think this will work," she said, and she started tugging.

As she tugged, I simply hung my head—embarrassed because I couldn't get up myself and angry that she wouldn't help me in an effective way. *Just get me my phone,* I thought. My body jerked as she fruitlessly tugged and tugged. I suppose she either expected me to miraculously stand up, or she just plain didn't understand that I couldn't walk.

She finally let go of my hand. I was relieved. *Now she at least knows there's not a simple fix.*

"It's okay," I said, trying to help her feel better about her useless, exasperating, futile effort. "My husband even has trouble picking me up straight from the ground—it's really hard. I'm dead weight, and I can't hold on very well."

I asked again for my phone, and she looked thoughtful. I tried to smile sweetly as she thought about getting me my phone, even though my mind was reeling. *I am so sure she needs to consider this request!*

"You know, my husband works really close," I said again, hoping to sound convincing. "You could even wait with me and keep me company until he gets here." Maybe she just needed something to do, I thought. "Will you please just hand me my phone?" I could tell she wasn't swayed, and it was starting to rain harder. And she was coming closer again.

I was getting desperate. "Please," I said, "just hand me my phone. He will be here in a second!" I could see I was getting nowhere by asking for my phone. "Or go inside!" I exclaimed. "Go inside and grab somebody—anybody—to come out and help us." I was hoping that the somebody else would also be reasonable and get me my phone.

But this wrinkled, old (and probably deaf) woman came even closer and proceeded to straddle my legs. She bent down and shoved her skinny, wrinkled hands into my armpits, and then she started to count.

"One," she said with a shaky, old voice.

I couldn't believe it. I stared up at her. Was she kidding?

"Two."

I closed my eyes and hung my head—bracing myself—because I knew she was going to fall on top of me.

"Three!"

What happened next is still a little difficult for me to believe, but the power of service continues to amaze me. No matter how hard it is raining in your life, you are strongest when you reach down to pick up someone else.

And I tell you that that small, wrinkled, frail, old woman singlehandedly picked me up and shoved me into the car. Then she turned around and walked back into her own storm.

> Savior may I learn to love thee,
> Walk the path that thou hast shown,
> Pause to help and lift another,
> Finding strength beyond my own.[40]

It rains on all of us. Some days it is just a little drizzle, and other days we wade through knee-deep floods and have no umbrella. But if we look through the drops, we will see those who are sitting in deeper puddles than our own. We may not think we have enough strength to help them—after all, our own troubles are many—but if we are willing to forget ourselves and reach down with everything we have and start counting, the Lord will make up what we lack. We will be strong enough to lift them out of their puddles and stronger as we turn around and face our own storms.

It is easy to serve and lift others out of their storms. Freshly baked cookies or fanfare or elaborate gifts and cards are not necessary to serve. We don't have to involve others to perform detailed and complex service projects in our neighborhoods and communities. We don't have to coordinate our efforts with anyone else's to perform a notable service, worthy of praise. President Monson said that each of us is surrounded by service opportunities.[41]

If all we have is a friendly face and a moment to appear as if we have nothing to do, we have enough to serve a friend in need, and those short acts of service have lasting consequences for both the giver and receiver.

An old friend from my senior year of high school contacted me on Facebook. We had lost touch, but in a short message, she said, "Oh, Meg, I am so excited to have found you! I have been

---

40   "Lord, I Would Follow Thee," Hymn no. 220.
41   "What Have I Done for Someone Today?" *Ensign*, November 2009.

looking for you everywhere. I'll never forget the day we met in high school when you invited me to eat lunch with you and your friends."

I don't even remember that day ten years ago. I don't remember asking her to eat lunch with us. I just remember that we were friends. What a small and forgettable thing for me, but what a memorable event for her.

I did not have many friends in high school. I wasn't popular. I even felt like the storms raged every day as I walked the halls at school, most of the time alone. But in my thirst to *have* friends, I quenched the thirst of others and *was* a friend. Then none of us thirsted anymore.

As we serve others, we are blessed in return. Blessings from heaven truly will surround us for our efforts. As we serve others, we will help relieve their thirsts and forget our own. We will be the answers to their prayers and the catalysts of our own strength and happiness.

### The Gaps of Life

As we work to close the gaps, we can't let Satan sneak his grabby hand through any tiny space to pull us down. We must be constantly grateful, have an eternal attitude, converse with Heavenly Father through prayer and scripture study, and serve. Nothing can be left out of our everyday efforts. President Ezra Taft Benson said, "There has never been more expected of the faithful in such a short period of time as there is of us. . . . Each day we personally make many decisions that show where our support will go."[42] We are sidestepping off our path with every effort that is not directly in support of the Savior.

The devil is watching us every single day to see if we will forget any of the steps to closing the gaps—anything seemingly small, like ingratitude, judgmental thoughts, not praying, and not serving can be detrimental. He wants us spiritually paralyzed. The decisions we make every day can either keep Satan below the

---

42 "In His Steps," *Speeches,* March 4, 1979.

rocks or leave enough room for us to fall through. Speaking about the decisions we make daily, President Uchtdorf said that major consequences are brought on by minor decisions.[43]

Once we let ourselves become spiritually paralyzed, we will be less able to feel the promptings of the Spirit. The Lord will seem far away. Because we are down with Satan in the cracks, we cannot progress on our journey. The difficulties of life will surround us, and we will feel every sharp rock and rough patch as we struggle in the dark crevices of life.

We don't become crimson sinners right away; it takes only a small—even tiny—wrong decision to lead us totally off course. There was a time in my life when I did not value the commandments of the Lord in a way that would bless my life. I was active in the Church, and I read my scriptures, but I was too casual with my social activities, and I became, for a brief time, spiritually paralyzed.

It was while I lived and worked in Florida. I loved being down there, and I got involved with a social crowd that frequented night clubs. Many people in the club were drinking and smoking, but *I* wasn't. Many people were talking coarsely and swearing, but *I* wasn't talking that way. Many people were dancing dirty, but *I* wasn't dancing that way. I was just there.

After one long night at the club with my friends, I returned home exhausted. I got into my pajamas and threw my smoke-smelling clothes into the dirty clothes pile. I knelt by my bed and prayed. In my prayer, I asked Heavenly Father a question I had been asking Him for quite a few days. It's been many years since this night, and I can't even remember my question, but I will never forget the answer.

Through the scriptures, the Lord told me that He was not going to answer me.

As I read my scriptures, the Spirit's peace confirmed to my heart that the Lord was speaking to me as I read the words, "Inasmuch as they are faithful unto me, it shall be made known unto them what they shall do."[44]

---

43 "A Matter of a Few Degrees," *Ensign*, May 2008.
44 D&C 52:4.

I was not being faithful to the commandments the Lord had given me, and because I was not being faithful, I would not receive the revelation I sought. At the top of the page, I read the words I had written in a seminary class a few years earlier, "Why do you do what you do when you know what you know?"

I was spiritually paralyzed. I had been casual in my social interactions and had caused the gaps surrounding me to widen. I'd allowed Satan to pull me down, and because I had done that, I could not progress on my path or receive the spiritual direction I needed.

We all get lazy sometimes and make mistakes. But the celestial kingdom won't be empty; it will be filled with people like you and me, who make mistakes but repent and better themselves little by little. And unlike physical paralysis, spiritual paralysis can be cured.

If we relax in our efforts to close the gaps and we get pulled down, we can repent and make the everyday choices that will close those gaps and squish Satan so we can get back on the path.

We are so blessed to be able to repent! We all make mistakes, and the Lord has made it possible for us to be forgiven. When we sin we feel dirty and, well, paralyzed. We don't feel like singing or reading our scriptures or praying because, like Elder Clate Mask Jr. said, "We don't want to stand before the Lord looking muddy."[45] But when we repent, we have a skip in our step that makes this life feel refreshed and clean.

We become muddy from committing "small" sins, like telling white lies and swearing, and from large sins, like immorality. The mud stays with us, and we feel dirty and cloaked in the mess we have made.

Before I was paralyzed, I had never sat in a wheelchair. Before I was paralyzed, I had never even known anyone in a wheelchair. The only connection to the wheelchair community I had was from the Bountiful Utah Temple open house in 1994—I'd been part of the group that gave the wheelchair tours. Little did I know

---

45   "Standing Spotless before the Lord," *Ensign*, May 2004.

that eleven years later, I would come back to that temple to receive my endowment—in my *own* wheelchair.

At first, I was awkward in my wheelchair. I didn't know how to push it straight or fast or hardly at all. I didn't want to look awkward in my chair, so I practiced. I committed that I would push up and down my front sidewalk at least once a day.

My front sidewalk wasn't a regular sidewalk next to the road. I had a small walkway/sidewalk connecting my front porch to the street sidewalk. It was a wheelchair friendly path, or it was intended to be.

My family had made a lot of changes to our house when I was in the hospital so I could come home and live there comfortably. One of these changes was the front porch and sidewalk. My mom didn't want the sidewalk to look too "straight," as if a disabled person lived there, so she had it made to look as if a disabled person could *never* live there. She had the cement squares wind from side to side up the slight hill in the front yard, like an *S*.

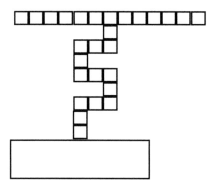

Pushing up and down this sidewalk each day was a very hard exercise for me because I had puny little arms and a heavy wheelchair. What made it even harder was the fact that the sidewalk went up a small hill. Going up was difficult because I had to use every bit of my strength. I could barely breathe when I did it. Once at the top, I had to rest a moment before I could come back down. You might think that coming back down the sidewalk would be easy, but it isn't. To go down a hill, I have to squeeze my wheels hard with both hands so I don't go too fast. This makes turning hard and breathing harder.

During this newly paralyzed time of my life, my little nephew was always with me. He was just three years old, and he was my best little helper. He would reach things for me by climbing onto my lap and getting on the counter, and he would help me push my wheelchair when I was tired (though he couldn't see over it). I remember when he first realized I was on wheels. I was barely out of the hospital, and he wanted me to come and look at something. He had a speech impediment and was unable to pronounce the *K* sound, so I heard, "Meg, t'mere. Meg, t'mere. Meg, t'mere . . ."

I was trying to ignore him because I was tired and didn't want to "come here." After what seemed like several minutes, he stopped. I was glad for the silence. Then I started to roll backwards—I looked behind my chair to see my little nephew pulling me to where he wanted me to "tome."

I loved being with my nephew. He was always excited for me when I did something by myself. Even though he was young, I think he understood the difficulty of what I was doing.

One morning when I went out practicing on the front sidewalk, it was very rainy. My nephew came outside with me but stayed out of the rain under the covered porch while I pushed up the sidewalk. My dad had been planting flowers next to the sidewalk—only there weren't flowers yet—and the entire walkway was surrounded by mud.

I pushed my hardest through the rain. It actually felt nice because it wasn't as hot as I expended the effort it took to get to the top. Once there, I turned around and squeezed tightly on my wheels with my wrists and started to go down. I tried to not let my wheelchair pick up a lot of speed so I could control it. I turned right, then left, then right again.

I must have felt a little overconfident in my turning abilities because at the very last turn, I was too close to the edge of the sidewalk. I wasn't able to turn enough, and the front wheel of my chair hung over the edge of the concrete above the mud.

I tried to lean back in my chair to pull the wheel back up the hill, but I wasn't strong enough. I teetered over the edge, my little wheel wobbling on top of the mud. I tried to call for help, but I was using all my strength to keep myself on the sidewalk; I couldn't find the breath to cry out.

My strength weakened, and the little, tiny wheel landed on top of the mud. The momentum of the forward fall sunk the wheel deeper into the mud, and then the whole wheelchair fell forward, dumping me out.

I landed face first. In the mud.

The wheelchair landed on top of me, squishing me farther into the mud, then fell to the side of me.

I started to cry, and my nephew came running and said in his broken speech, "Meg! Meg! You o'tay? You o'tay? You trying?" I told him that I was okay. Yes, I was crying, but it was okay.

Had my nephew been sufficiently strong, he would have picked me up, cleaned off the mud, and righted me on my wheelchair and back on the sidewalk. He was there for me.

As we journey through this life, we will take side steps off the path and get a little dirty, a little dusty, and a little muddy. But the good news is that we all have a special friend, like my nephew, who stands by us as we travel, shouts words of encouragement, and helps us when we're failing. That friend is Jesus Christ.

He watches over us and knows how close we are to the edge, and He *is* strong enough to pull us out of the mud when we ask for His help. He will clear us of all the caked-on dirt and grime and mud and set us back on the path. As we follow the Savior's commandment to "repent . . . that ye may stand spotless before me,"[46] we will come to recognize His help in keeping us spiritually able.

When we repent, we will know what the prodigal son must have felt like as he returned home without his inheritance, without his pride, without anything at all. When his father saw him coming, his father ran—he *ran*—to meet him.[47] When we repent and turn away from our sins and come back to the Lord and follow His commandments, we will feel the Savior *running* to meet us too.

---

46    3 Nephi 27:20.
47    Luke 15:11–32.

There are countless ways to get dirty, dusty, and muddy, but only one way to become clean. We all have layers of mud and dust to wash away—whether it's because we've done something we know we shouldn't or because we've *not* done something we know we should have. Washing away those grimy layers is how we become spiritually "able." Elder Neil L. Andersen taught, "I speak of marvelous spiritual feelings that come through the gift of the Savior's atonement as the layers of sin are washed away and we come to feel spiritually clean."[48] We can feel clean and have forgiveness as we get back on the path and feel the Savior's love. The Savior always loves us—muddy or clean—but it's only when we *feel* clean that we can *feel* His love also.

Keeping clean from the dusty, everyday journey is not easy. There are temptations everywhere to commit sin and omit righteousness.

Remember Daniel and the lions' den? King Nebuchadnezzar loved Daniel and promoted him to be one of his counselors, but the other counselors were jealous of Daniel and tried to turn the king against him. These wicked counselors knew Daniel loved the Lord and prayed every day, so they tricked the king into signing a law stating that no one could pray or worship any god except the king. If anyone did, they would be thrown into the lions' den.[49]

*The lions' den.* Can you imagine being thrown into a pit with hungry lions? Me neither.

Daniel knew about the law—and about the punishment. But still, he prayed. He didn't even try to be sneaky about it; he prayed right in front of the window. Sometimes I wonder what he prayed for. I bet it had something to do with not being eaten by lions.

But regardless of *what* he prayed for, he didn't know he would be miraculously saved. He didn't know God would shut the mouths of the lions and he would be okay. He didn't know. Daniel was prepared to be eaten by lions.

Like Daniel, we don't know what will happen when we choose to stay on our path. The lions litter our everyday trail as Satan tempts

48 "The Joy of Becoming Clean," *Ensign,* April 1995.
49 Daniel 6:4–27.

us to commit sin and omit righteousness—anything to make us side step into spiritual paralysis. Sometimes our friends and family are swayed into the gaps. Spiritually paralyzed friends and family members encourage us to join them in their actions and accept their philosophies. While we love them, we can't do either without risking our own spiritual ability. Satan uses those we love as modern-day lions to scare us into relinquishing some of our spiritual ability.

Even as we stand tall spiritually against the unrighteous encouragement coming from those around us, sometimes God won't close the mouths of the lions. Sometimes He will let them taunt us. Sometimes He will let them hate us. Sometimes He will let them eat us. Even if we choose not to commit a sin or not to omit righteousness, we often don't know how these modern-day lions will react.

Say you are sitting with your entire extended family in a movie theater or in the audience of a play, and all of a sudden, the dialogue turns nasty. You realize this entertainment doesn't coincide with your standards, but you don't know if it's a passing scene or if the entire show will be that way . . .

What should you do?

You know the obvious Primary answer, but you don't want to be rude! Plus, you've paid for your ticket, and it was pricey. No one in your family seems to be bothered, and you're sitting in the middle of the row.

As a modern-day Daniel, you have two places to pray—hidden in your closet or right in front of the window. Sometimes it is right to pray in your closets, but in this instance, being subtle about your standards and still keeping them—like closing your eyes during the bad scenes—may not be enough. But if you "pray in front of the window" and stand up in the middle of the show to crawl over everyone in the audience to get out, people might not be too happy with you.

Sometimes when we "pray in front of our window," we're considered arrogant and self-righteous. Sometimes our friends won't understand our standards. Sometimes our family will be angry at us for reminding them of our standards. God doesn't always close their mouths.

Sometimes those who see our righteous example are not softened. Sometimes they are hardened against us. The wicked people of Ammonihah would not believe the gospel the prophet Alma and Amulek taught. They took the wives and children of those who believed the gospel and cast them into a fire—burning them to death.

As the women and children cried out, Amulek asked Alma, "How can we witness this awful scene? . . . let us stretch forth our hands . . . and save them from the flames." But Alma said that he could not because the Lord "doth suffer that they may do this thing, or that the people may do this thing unto them, according to the hardness of their hearts."[50]

The fires burned those righteous women and children. Likewise, we are not always saved from the flames. Daniel was saved from the hungry lions, but we won't always be.

Is that enough to stop us?

As modern-day Daniels, what do we say in our prayers? Do we ask that the lions' mouths will be closed? Or do we ask for thicker skin?

As Joshua led the Israelites, he was worried that he would not be a good enough leader, but the Lord consoled him by saying, "Be strong and of a good *courage*; be not afraid, neither be thou dismayed: for the Lord thy God is with thee whithersoever thou goest."[51]

I love the word *courage*. To me, courage is not the same as bravery. When we're brave, we are fearless and confident. But I rarely feel that way. Like you, I know people who dislike it when I pray at my window. I fear that those lions may eat me and that the fires will burn me—but I fear God more. In my fear, I have little room for bravery.

But I have room for courage. Courage is not the absence of fear. Rather, it is the willingness and determination to do what needs doing anyway—*despite* how we feel. With courage, we can fall down on our knees right in front of our window, standing tall in our commitment to righteousness, and let the lions eat us.

---

50  Alma 14:10–11.
51  Joshua 1:9; emphasis added.

With courage, we can walk through the fires that burn, and as we do, we will walk with God. As we are courageous, we will know that if lions eat us, we're going to taste good because the fruits of the Spirit are sweet!

So let the lions eat us as we bear our testimony with our actions and pray in front of our windows. Let the fires burn us to a standard-waving crisp! There is nothing on our trail—no lion, no fire, no rock—that we can't handle when we walk with God, even if we can't walk.

Let us start closing the gaps with gratitude, even—and especially—when it feels like we have nothing left to be grateful for. Let us have an eternal attitude and remember that we were excited for this life—trials and all. Let us have conversations with the Lord through prayer and scripture study. Let us serve. Carrying others' burdens will make ours light.

Close the gaps. Though our path will not be smooth, our spiritually abilities will be increased.

As we close the gaps, we will come to know the truth of Sister Becky Thomas's words, "As we begin to close those gaps, we will experience the true love of Christ."[52] Jesus Christ loves us. He knows where we are. He knows what has happened to us. And He knows what will happen to us. As we travel down our path, He will walk with us.

As long as I can walk with God, it doesn't matter that I can't literally walk. I know Joseph Smith saw Heavenly Father and Jesus Christ in the Sacred Grove, and because I know this, I know that someday I will see Them too. And on that day, I will stand.

And I will stand tall.

---

52 "Closing the Gap—How We Live Our Lives vs. What We Believe," *Deseret News* Archives, December 6, 2009.

# About the Author

Artist and author Meg Johnson continues to motivate thousands of people across the globe with her motto, "When life gets too hard to stand, just keep on rollin'!" Meg accidentally jumped off a cliff and broke her neck in 2004 and spent four months in the hospital recovering from multiple injuries. She returned home without the use of her legs, back, stomach, or hands—a quadriplegic. Meg knows that even though being physically paralyzed is hard, being spiritually paralyzed is harder. This book details the steps we can take to remain spiritually able.

Since being paralyzed, Meg has competed in the national Ms. Wheelchair America pageant in New York, founded and directed Ms. Wheelchair Utah (and still directs it), and instituted a service outreach program for recovering hospital patients. Meg reaches peoples' hearts worldwide through her newsletter, *Meg's Monthly Message: A True Story from My Life to Help You in Yours.* She received the Athena Award in 2012 for her service efforts. She enjoys her greatest accomplishment every day as she gets to be a wife to her husband, Whit.

To meet Meg, watch her videos, listen to free audio, or sign up for her newsletter, visit her on her website, www.MegJohnsonSpeaks.com. Meg also has a talk on CD, *When Life Gets Hard* . . ., available in bookstores.